Just Let Go

Jamie Morrison

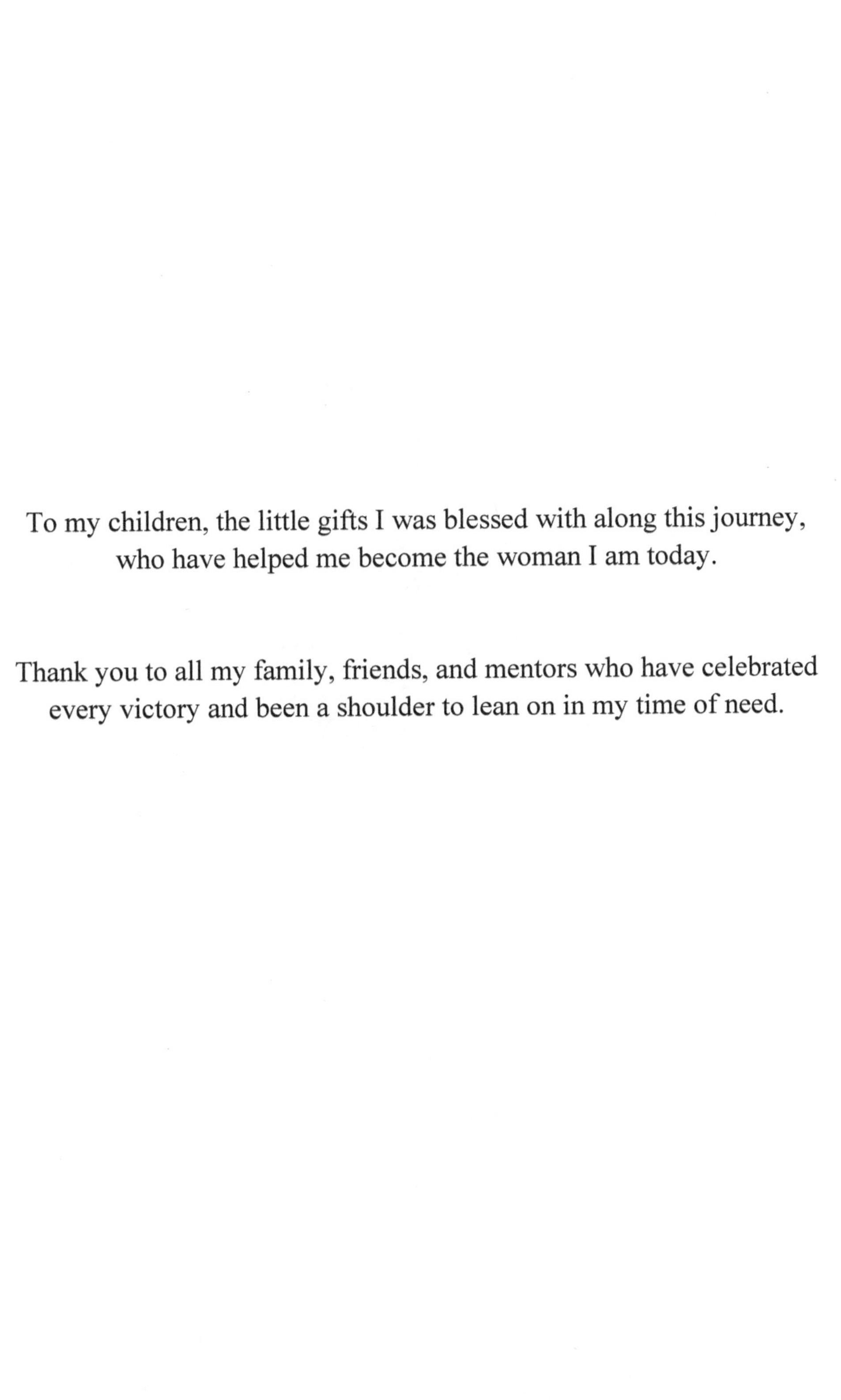

To my children, the little gifts I was blessed with along this journey, who have helped me become the woman I am today.

Thank you to all my family, friends, and mentors who have celebrated every victory and been a shoulder to lean on in my time of need.

TABLE OF CONTENTS

Preface
The Weight We Carry

Being a Black woman in America means living at the crossroads of two identities long marginalized, misunderstood, and overburdened. It means moving through a world that too often refuses to see us clearly, yet demands everything from us – our labor, our brilliance, our culture, our strength – without offering safety, tenderness, or rest in return. From the moment we arrive, the world projects its expectations, its fears, and its fantasies onto us. We are told to be strong, yet not too loud; resilient, yet never angry; ambitious, yet always grateful. We are expected to endure, to lead, to nurture, to fight, but rarely to simply be.

We carry our families, our communities, and our histories on our backs. We inherit both pain and perseverance, trauma and triumph. Our grandmothers may not have had the luxury to cry. Our mothers may have been too busy surviving to dream. Still, here we are, trying to create something new from the bones of what we were given. Somewhere beneath all that weight, beneath the layers of responsibility, identity, and survival, we are simply trying to remember who we are. Who we were before the world told us what to be. Who we were before we learned to shrink, to hustle, to protect, to perform. This book is born from that remembering. It is a homecoming. It is a soft place to land. It is a sanctuary carved from the truth of our lived experiences.

"Just Let Go" is more than just a title; it's a heartfelt prayer passed down through generations. It serves as a defiance against the notion that we must always be everything for everyone. This work is a roadmap back to our true selves and a love letter to every Black woman who has questioned her worth.

While it tells my story, it is also a collective narrative. It captures the process of shedding layers of generational trauma that taught us to persist regardless of the circumstances; layers of societal conditioning that trained us to earn love through self-sacrifice; and layers of personal pain that we often never allowed ourselves to acknowledge or feel.

This is a story of unlearning the habits of continually proving, performing, and protecting. It is about the journey of discovering how to embrace love fully, freely, and unapologetically.

This process of letting go is not easy. It is not about abandoning responsibility or pretending pain never happened. It is about choosing softness where there was once only steel, choosing presence over perfection. It is about allowing ourselves to feel, to rest, to grieve, to celebrate. It is about telling the truth, first to ourselves, then to the world. We are tired. We deserve better. We are already whole.

For many years, I believed I needed to earn rest, love, and softness. I thought that by working diligently, loving fiercely, remaining silent, and constantly proving my worth, I would eventually feel complete. I thought wholeness would arrive like a reward for my suffering, but healing taught me something different, something sacred. Wholeness isn't earned; it's remembered. It was never lost, only buried beneath the noise. We were born worthy, sacred, and whole. The world just made us forget.

In these pages, I invite you into the mess and the magic of what it means to be a Black woman reclaiming herself. You'll walk with me through heartbreak and healing, through ambition and burnout, through fear and faith. You'll see what it looks like to find your voice in boardrooms that try to silence you, to choose love after betrayal, to build wealth in a world designed to keep you broke, and to reconnect with the divine, not through dogma, but through your own sacred knowing. This journey isn't linear, and it's not always gentle, but it is always yours.

This book holds space for the laughter that breaks through sorrow, the joy that surprises us in our quietest moments, and the power that rises when we dare to say yes to ourselves. It is a witness to our complexities, a mirror for our beauty, and a call to live fully. We are allowed to be soft and strong, to rest and rise, to speak and stay silent, to love and protect our peace. We are allowed to define ourselves on our own terms.

More than anything, I hope you find yourself in these pages. Not the version of you shaped by the world's expectations, but the You that existed before the world told you to change. I hope you find the courage to let go of the pain, the pressure, and the perfectionism. To soften. To open. To embrace the life that has always been waiting for you, where you don't have to hustle for your worth and where joy is not a reward but a right: the life where you get to be free.

When we let go, we rise. And when we rise, we lift generations with us. When we heal, we change the story for those who come after us. When we come home to ourselves, we become a light in a world that desperately needs it.

So, take a breath, sis. Take off your armor. Come home to yourself. This is your permission to be free. You don't have to earn it; just remember it. Let this be the beginning of your return.

Part 1

THE ARMOR WE WEAR

"Before we can let go, we must first acknowledge what we've been holding."

This part of the book explores the emotional, cultural, and societal armor Black women are taught to wear from the earliest moments of childhood: armor meticulously built to guard against the sharp edges of racism, sexism, classism, and rejection. It is the armor passed down through generations: the look of composure when we're breaking inside, the readiness to fight and protect at all costs, the silence in rooms where our brilliance is ignored or appropriated. We are taught, both directly and silently, that survival depends on being impenetrable.

We don't always realize when the armor is being fitted. Sometimes it begins with a mother's warning before school: "You have to be twice as good." Other times, it's a sideways glance from a teacher when our voice carries too far. It's the early lesson that softness is a risk, that tears are a luxury we can't afford, that our anger will always be seen as aggression and never as grief. Slowly, silently, we begin to build the wall, stone by stone. We smile when we want to cry. We achieve when we want to rest. We become what the world demands while tucking away the fullness of who we are.

While this armor may shield us from harm, it also seals us off from what is most tender and necessary: softness, rest, intimacy, vulnerability, and the kind of love that sees us fully and doesn't demand performance in return. It distances us from our own emotional truths, numbing us to the ache within because we're too busy managing the expectations outside. We learn to equate strength with repression, success with hardship, and love with perseverance. We become fluent in excellence but mute in our own emotional languages. We know how to show up for everyone, yet we forget how to show up for ourselves.

These chapters peel back those layers. They ask us to examine the ways we've internalized the myths of invincibility, the Strong

Black Woman narrative, which praises our endurance but rarely honors our pain, celebrating our ability to survive while overlooking our right to thrive. They ask us to reflect on the price of perfectionism and the quiet grief of being everything to everyone but never enough to ourselves. The grief of never having been allowed to fall apart, applauded for carrying so much when what we really needed was someone to help us put it down.

We confront the ways we've made homes out of hyper-independence, made peace with burnout, and confused boundaries with walls. We name the survival strategies we've mistaken for personality traits. We reckon with the guilt we feel for even wanting more: more rest, more ease, more softness, more joy. And in that reckoning, we begin to remember ourselves. Not the polished, perfected version but the tender, true, imperfect self that's always existed beneath the armor.

At this moment, let's take a step back and ponder: What burdens are we shouldering? Whose expectations are we conforming to? What would it feel like to safely remove our masks? To be embraced without needing to explain ourselves? To be loved unconditionally? How might our lives transform if we no longer had to display strength as a measure of our value?

This is a homecoming to our humanity, a tender reckoning, a soft, sacred invitation to be real, vulnerable, and free. It is an invitation to remember that we are not machines, saviors, or symbols. We are human beings, worthy of care, deserving of joy, and entitled to rest. The truest liberation begins not in resistance, but in release. In that release, we don't lose our power; we find it, we reclaim it, we embody it, not through force, but through truth, through presence, through love.

Chapter 1
BORN INTO BATTLE

"Before I ever knew who I was, I knew I had to protect her."

We don't get to enter this world gently, not as Black girls in America. We're taught the world isn't a soft place for us. We're taught how to shrink, how to survive, and how to shine just enough to be seen, but never so much that we become a threat. The lessons are unspoken but deeply understood. Be polite, but not too assertive. Be smart, but don't outshine. Be strong, but never vulnerable. These quiet rules are written into our lives before we even understand the language of power, race, or gender.

I remember being six years old, sitting in a classroom where I was the only black girl. My hand shot up, eager and full of light, curiosity bubbling in my chest like soda fizzing to the top. But the teacher looked past me. She called on someone else. Then someone else again. My arm, once stretched with hope, slowly dropped. My voice, once loud with wonder, grew quiet. I didn't have the words then to name what was happening, but I felt it deep in my body. That was the beginning of disappearing, of learning that visibility came with conditions and that worthiness wasn't something I could count.

It wasn't just in the classroom. It followed me everywhere: in the subtle glances telling me I didn't belong, the way people stared at my natural hair like it was something to fear or tame. It showed up in the way people talked over me in conversations, as if my thoughts needed confirmation to be valid. I saw it in the way I was expected to carry emotional weight far beyond my years, to be composed, mature, and responsible before I ever had the chance to just be a child. I was told to smile, be graceful under pressure, and never let them see me sweat, even when I was drowning.

These moments, small and relentless, taught me something: Black girls are not granted the same softness, the same safety, the same space to grow. We are forced to grow armor before we even know what we're protecting ourselves from. And yet, even as we're silenced, overlooked, or misunderstood, we keep rising, quietly powerful, beautifully complex, and wholly deserving of a different way to be.

The First Messages We Receive

The messages arrive early. Stay strong. Don't show tears. Avoid complaining. Don't falter. Remain quiet. Limit your words. Question softly. Don't occupy too much space. Strive for improvement. Work twice as hard. Be twice as talented. Avoid giving them any reason to doubt, fear, or dismiss you. Be thankful for what you receive, even when it's insufficient, even when it causes pain. Exercise caution. With your body. With your tone. With your aspirations. With your presence. Every word, every step, every breath is scrutinized for survival. These messages are not delivered gently; they are passed down like instructions or doctrine. They are whispered by concerned mothers, echoed by weary teachers, and affirmed by a world that expects Black girls to mature quickly while demanding little. They influence our self-worth before we even recognize who we are, teaching us that acceptance comes at the cost of being small, silent, and exceptional. Long before we comprehend the meaning of true freedom, we are already learning the art of endurance.

These words arrive long before we have the language to question them. Long before we understand their weight or where they come from. They are whispered in our ears, echoed in the way our tears are met with discomfort, and woven into the rules we are expected to follow before we even know who we are. These messages become our first lessons in survival. We internalize them, memorize them, and perform them. And with each repetition, a part of our softness folds inward, hidden for safekeeping.

We are taught to anticipate pain before we even know what joy fully feels like. Our childhood is often cut short, not just by the responsibilities we're given but by the armor we're taught to wear. That armor looks like overachievement. It looks like silence. It looks like becoming "the good one," "the smart one," or "the one who never cries." We learn early that being exceptional might buy us safety, that being quiet might protect us from harm, and that hiding our emotions might help us survive a world that isn't built to hold our tenderness.

We become experts at reducing ourselves to fit into the molds others created for us. We smile when we want to scream. We say yes when everything in us aches to say no. We push ourselves to exhaustion, hoping someone will finally see how much we're carrying. But often, no one does. Or if they do, they call it strength. They celebrate our ability to keep going, never asking if we're okay, never considering what it's costing us to be everything to everyone.

For many of us, there's also the unspoken trauma that lives inside our homes. We grow up watching our mothers carry weight without complaint, moving through life with a strength that looks effortless but costs everything. We learn, not through words but through their worn bodies and tired eyes, that rest is a luxury and vulnerability is dangerous. We learn to do the same. We inherit silence, we inherit resilience, we inherit pain that no one ever talks about – not because our mothers didn't love us, but because they didn't know how to let go either. They were doing what they were taught, passing down the only tools they had. And so, the cycle continues until we dare to break it.

Breaking the cycle doesn't always look revolutionary at first. Sometimes, it looks like crying in the shower because you don't know how to ask for help. It looks like choosing therapy over silence. It looks like turning down another obligation because your body is begging you to rest. It looks like saying, "I don't want to do this anymore," even when you're not sure what comes next. It's messy. It's hard. It often comes with guilt, but it is a sacred experience.

I remember when I found myself at this pivotal moment of understanding, confronted with the decision to either continue the cycle or create a new path. This choice was challenging, as change is seldom easy, especially when the patterns we carry have been deeply ingrained over generations. Yet, as I stood at the edge of potential, unsure and trembling, I began to comprehend the quiet strength found in vulnerability and the power that lives in gentleness. I started to realize courage isn't always loud or fierce; sometimes, it's the quiet voice at the end of the day, softly saying, "I will try again tomorrow."

That whisper became my anthem, a reminder that persistence wrapped in tenderness is still strength.

As I leaned into this new understanding, I discovered that joy, in its most genuine and transformative form, emerges when I allow myself to be fully seen, known, and loved for who I truly am, with all my imperfections included. It does not demand perfection, nor does it require me to earn my worthiness. I recognized authentic connection is born not from performance but from presence, sharing our stories, opening our hearts to others, and daring to be genuine in a world that often prioritizes masks over truth and conformity over individuality.

With this awakening, I set out to redefine our narrative. I began to unlearn the rigid lessons of silence and self-sacrifice, instead learning to celebrate the small, quiet victories that once went unnoticed. I started to appreciate the beauty hidden within the failures, the wisdom born from surrender, and the grace found in every attempt to rise again. I came to understand that it is not only acceptable but necessary to rest, to feel deeply, and to seek help. There is courage in softness, strength in leaning, and power in receiving. I began to honor the legacy of resilience passed down by my foremothers while also making space for tenderness, laughter, and dreams that had been deferred for too long.

Sometimes, I still hear those early messages echoing in the background: Be strong. Be quiet. Be better. But now, I respond with something new: Be soft. Be honest. Be free. Be whole. I speak to the little Black girl inside me who was once told survival meant hiding. I tell her we have a new goal: liberation. And liberation means loving ourselves out loud, without shame, without apology, and without conditions.

In this journey of returning to myself, I not only healed parts of my own soul but also forged a path reaching beyond me, a pathway for future generations to walk unburdened by inherited silence. I became one of the architects of a new story, a new way of being, one where love, hope, and compassion are not distant ideals but living, breathing truths. In doing so, I learned that letting go is not about losing, but about finding freedom. It is the act of reclaiming everything we were told to suppress. It is the beginning of becoming whole.

Carrying Generations

As Black women, we don't just carry our own stories: we carry generations. We carry grandmothers who never got to rest, whose hands bore the weight of labor without recognition, whose dreams were tucked away for the sake of survival. We carry mothers who survived what they could never speak aloud, who wore silence like armor and pain like a second skin. We carry the daughters we're trying to protect from what once broke us, pouring into them the love, wisdom, and strength we had to gather piece by piece.

We carry it all: grief and grace, strength and sorrow, hope and heartbreak, folded into our bodies and woven into our daily lives. This inheritance is invisible to most, yet evident in the way we walk into a room. It lingers in the furrow of our brows, the arch of our backs, the pause before we speak our truths. It hums beneath our laughter and echoes in the tears we don't always have the space to shed.

Because of this, our identities are shaped as much by defense as by desire. We are often molded by necessity before we are nurtured by possibility. The world hands us responsibility before it offers us freedom. We often don't get to ask, *"Who am I?"* because we are too busy answering, *"How do I survive?"* Survival becomes the script we memorize long before we get to write our own story. Our sense of self is often born not from exploration but from endurance, making a way where there was none, holding it all together when everything inside us was coming undone.

We grow up quickly. I was barely a seasoned first grader and I remember having to care for my six-month-old sister so that my mother could provide. I would wake myself up in the early hours of the morning, get myself ready, get her ready, carefully brushing her baby hair into little puffs, then walk her to daycare with small, determined steps. I didn't know then I was carrying something sacred and heavy at the same time. I had no grasp of what it meant to grow up too quickly, weighed down by responsibilities far beyond my years. There were no words for the exhaustion or the quiet pride I carried.

Responsibilities such as these teach us to persevere very early on – not because we were told to but because we needed to. Because love, especially in Black families, often looks like sacrifice. Love isn't always soft or spoken. Sometimes it's a warm plate of food, a ride to work, a bill paid on time, even if it meant something else had to wait. We were driven by love and moved for the sake of family, doing what had to be done without complaint. There is no luxury in lingering innocence when the world demands so much from us so soon. We adapt, rise, and endure, even when the weight of it is never fully acknowledged. Even when no one says thank you. We learn to read a room before we read a book, sensing shifts in tone, posture, and presence with intuitive precision. We know how to make ourselves small to avoid being seen as a threat, how to code-switch without even thinking, how to soften our truths so others don't feel too uncomfortable. We know how to switch our tone to sound less "aggressive," smoothing out our voices even when our truths burn inside. We know how to carry ourselves in a way that says, *"I belong,"* even when no one wants us there, even when we have to build our belonging from scratch. We know how to navigate systems not made for us, shapeshifting, shrinking, expanding, doing whatever it takes just to feel safe. Just to survive the day. That knowing runs deep. It's not learned from textbooks or classrooms. It's passed down in glances, warnings, prayers whispered beneath breath, and stories told between hair braids and kitchen counters.

This knowing is both our superpower and our scar tissue. It protects us and it burdens us. It keeps us safe but it also keeps us tired. It's what got us here, but it's not what will carry us forward. Even as we carry all this, we begin to ask new questions. Not just how to survive, but how to live. *How to be.* How to rest without guilt. How to dream without restraint. How to speak without shrinking. How to open our hands and release what was never ours to hold in the first place, the guilt, the pressure, the shame, the silence. The generational burdens we didn't agree to but carried anyway out of love, duty, and hope. We are the bridge between what was and what can be. The ones who still rise despite the weight. The ones daring to let the little girl inside us breathe again. The ones choosing to heal, to love, to rest, and to do so boldly. Healing ourselves means honoring those who came before us and freeing those who will come after.

The Toll of Constant Alertness

When your identity is forged in survival, joy becomes a luxury, vulnerability feels dangerous, rest feels like weakness, and freedom feels far away. We become so used to being on guard that we don't even realize we're holding our breath. Our nervous systems become wired to anticipate harm; our bodies quietly clench in preparation for impact that may never come but always feels just around the corner. It is time to release the residual trauma our bodies are carrying. It's about learning how to let our shoulders drop. To breathe all the way down into our bellies. It's about looking back, not with blame or shame, but with deep compassion for the girl we once were. The girl who tried to be perfect. The girl who kept showing up even when no one saw her. The girl who believed that if she just worked hard enough, they'd finally love her, respect her, and understand her. To her, I say: *You were never broken. You were responding to a broken world.*

A world that didn't make space for your fullness. A world that expected you to be twice as good for half the recognition. A world that praised your strength but ignored your wounds. You were doing the best you could with what you had, and that was more than enough.

It took me a long time to truly show up for myself. Vulnerability wasn't just uncomfortable, it was scary, like walking into a room naked and uncertain if you'll be embraced or exiled. For years, I kept my real feelings buried, tucked away beneath layers of silence and self-protection. I suspect fear began in childhood, when life taught me survival often meant suppressing my emotions.

At home, I carried responsibilities that didn't leave room for softness or play. I learned to clean up messes, both literal and emotional, before I ever learned how to name my own needs. Being a child came second to being useful, obedient, and composed. Beyond my front door, I was already navigating the unspoken burdens placed on me the moment I was born Black and a girl. I was taught to stand tall, to be twice as polite, to never let them see me cry.

I can still remember the early sting of judgment. The subtle stares from white classmates. I was overlooked, misunderstood, or dismissed before I even had the chance to speak. Those moments didn't just hurt, they planted quiet seeds of self-doubt that grew into vines of overachievement and self-erasure. I internalized the message that to be accepted, I had to be exceptional. To be safe, I had to be silent. Then there was the colorism within our own community, the offhand jokes meant to toughen us up but that quietly cut deep. The comments about skin tone, hair texture, and body shape. The constant need to prove our worth, not just to the outside world but within our own families and circles. In Black households, developing a thick skin is not optional. It's often considered a rite of passage, an armor they praise us for wearing even as it slowly suffocates our softer parts.

That armor, once instilled, stretches far beyond our homes and into every space we occupy: into classrooms where we're expected to outperform, workplaces where we're either invisible or under a microscope, relationships where we shrink ourselves to fit someone else's comfort. This need to be strong, to endure without complaint, becomes second nature. But strength without softness can harden into self-denial.

I didn't realize how deeply those scars shaped me. How they dictated my pace. How they fueled my perfectionism, the reason I never allowed myself to slow down, get comfortable, or risk failure. I was always alert, always scanning, always bracing for whatever might come next. Hypervigilance became my default, and for a long time, I mistook that for strength. I thought being constantly prepared meant being powerful. I thought not needing anyone meant being independent. I thought exhaustion was the price of success, but I was wrong.

Real strength allows space for softness, too. It doesn't live in the clenched jaw or the forced smile. It lives in the quiet decision to rest. In the brave act of asking for help. In the sacred moment, we let someone see us cry without apologizing.

This chapter is about learning to exhale, for the first time in years, or maybe ever. It's about stepping out of survival mode and into self-compassion. It's about honoring the ways we've coped, while gently choosing new ways to care for ourselves. It's about unlearning the lie that we have to earn our rest, our peace, our joy. We've been alert for so long. Now, it's time to come home to ease, to exhale, to be.

Letting Her Be Seen

As I begin this journey of letting go, I realize the first and perhaps most difficult thing I have to release is the belief I must constantly earn my worth. That belief has been with me for so long it began to almost feel like the truth, woven into my thoughts, stitched into my self-perception, embedded in my very way of being. It whispered to me in classrooms, echoed through corporate spaces where I worked twice as hard for half the recognition, and rang in relationships where I poured endlessly from an empty cup, hoping to be seen, chosen, and honored. That belief told me my value was conditional, based on how much I gave, how hard I worked, and how little I needed in return. It convinced me love must be earned, rest must be justified, and softness must be hidden.

But the deeper I travel into myself and the quieter I become, the more I listen and begin to hear a different, sacred voice. I begin to see the truth: I was always worthy. Even in my silence. Even in my sadness. Even in the moments I felt invisible or misunderstood. My worth was never up for negotiation, nor was it up for debate. It has always been whole, sacred, and mine. It was never in the hands of a teacher, a boss, a lover, or a parent. It was never a reward to be earned; it was a birthright, and I had it all along.

We all carry within us the little Black girl we once were, the one with a light in her eyes and dreams too big for the boxes the world tried to place her in. The one who wanted to be held without having to be strong first. The one who wanted to be listened to without being perfect. The one who wanted to dance without being watched, to speak without being silenced, to rest without being judged. The one who just wanted to be enough, exactly as she was. That little girl still lives within us, quietly waiting for permission to exhale. Waiting for the day she no longer has to perform to be loved. Waiting to come home, not to a physical place, but to herself.

This chapter is for her. It is an offering. A warm blanket for her tired spirit. A lullaby for her weary heart. A soft landing after years of bracing for impact. Because after all the surviving, all the striving, all the shrinking, we owe her our tenderness. We owe her our protection. We owe her our full attention. We owe her joy that isn't earned, laughter that isn't stifled, love that isn't transactional. It's time to let her breathe, to unclench the jaw and soften the shoulders, to feel sunlight on skin without looking over her shoulder. It's time to let her be, to laugh without apology, to rest without guilt, to take up space without fear. It's time make her feel at home. Not to a place, but to a knowing. A knowing she is already enough. That she is sacred. That she belongs. That she is the miracle, not the mistake.

Letting go isn't just about releasing pain. It's about reclaiming joy, peeling off the breastplate and remembering the softness that still lives underneath. It's about opening the door to freedom, not just for ourselves, but for every generation that comes after us. When we choose to honor the little girl within, when we finally tell her, "You are safe now," we change everything. We rewrite the story, healing not only ourselves but the lineages in our blood and the future in our breath. And we begin again, softly, freely, and whole.

Reflect on the roles you were handed before you even knew who you were. What expectations were placed on you to be strong, responsible, or resilient? Sit with the weight of those early assignments and ask yourself, did you choose them, or did they choose you? Are you still living by rules that were written for your survival, not your joy? Be honest about the cost of carrying those roles and consider what you might lay down if survival is no longer the only goal.

Chapter 2

THE SILENCE BETWEEN US

The unspoken rules we learn in Black households don't come from books; they are lived, absorbed, and inherited. They are stitched into our everyday lives like invisible threads: *don't cry, don't question, don't break.* These lessons are not always spoken aloud, but they're etched into the glances and careful avoidance of conversations that might unravel too much. Pain is acknowledged only in passing. Vulnerability is discouraged. And emotions, especially the tender ones, are tucked away behind a wall of strength.

I think of my grandmother, Nanny. That's what all the grandkids called her. She was the embodiment of resilience, a woman with a spine forged in fire and hands that had known labor since childhood. Nanny wasn't the kind to cuddle. Her love wasn't expressed in soft words or gentle touches. Her love was in her smile, in every piece of fruit she cut for me, and echoed in her constant motion. She had very strong feelings about emotions, especially the public display of them. To her, crying was not just unnecessary; it was uncomfortable. *"If it hasn't killed you, then you're okay,"* she would say. At the time, I thought she was being harsh, but now I understand those were survival words, likely passed down from her own grandmother, who raised her after her mother left. That abandonment, coupled with a childhood of picking cotton under the blistering southern sun and other traumas, taught her that silence was not only safer but also revered.

She spoke about the pain in her life in a matter-of-fact way, never letting emotion take up too much space. The violations, the betrayals, the grief: she recited them like a list, not a wound. That was her lesson. Don't dwell, don't look back, just keep going. She thought she was teaching me strength, and, in a way, she was, but I didn't realize until much later that she was also modeling a kind of compartmentalization that, while protective, can also become a cage. Her good intentions were wrapped in a covering I unknowingly inherited.

So many of us inherited this armor. We learned to wear that same mask: composed, capable, controlled. We didn't know we were absorbing generations of unresolved grief. We didn't know silence had become a love language passed down through necessity, that numbness had been mistaken for peace, that the absence of emotional expression had come to define what it meant to be "strong." We didn't know that what we were calling strength was, in some ways, a long-held trauma response.

The silence between us doesn't just reside in what was said, it resides in what was never spoken, the hugs not given, the apologies never offered, the softness never modeled. It lives in the discomfort we feel when we try to name our feelings out loud, unsure if anyone will receive them without judgment. That's what makes emotional avoidance its own kind of armor; it's a way of surviving without being seen and after a while that invisibility starts to feel normal, but normal doesn't mean healthy. Normal doesn't mean healed.

Now, as I learn to name my needs, to feel my feelings without shame, and to let myself cry, I still know I'm strong. I realize I'm not just healing for myself but for her, too, for the little girl who picked cotton and never knew softness. The woman who carried her pain in silence so her children wouldn't have to. All the Black women who were never given permission to fall apart. I'm breaking the silence, not to blame, but to breathe. Not to dishonor, but to release.

The silence between us ends with me, and with that ending comes a beginning, a chance to rewrite the rules, to welcome tenderness, to speak openly, to feel deeply. It serves as an invitation to reconnect with our true selves, not as the individuals we felt compelled to become, but as our authentic selves—complete, emotional, and liberated.

Inheriting Silence

In Black families, especially among the women, silence often passes from generation to generation like an heirloom. It's tucked into the folds of stories left untold, embedded in the pauses between what happened and what we're allowed to say out loud. We learn early – sometimes through words, more often through watching – that speaking our truth can come with consequences. So, we adapt. We observe how our mothers wipe away tears before anyone sees them fall. We notice how our grandmothers hold their pain in their backs, their hands, their swollen feet, but never in their voices. We watch aunties laugh too loudly at family gatherings, not because they're carefree, but because the alternative, crying or raging, might make them unravel. We learn that pushing forward, holding it in, and not making a scene is how you survive. That strength means silence. That dignity means discretion. That love means not talking about certain things.

Sometimes, these lessons aren't explicitly taught. Instead, they reveal themselves through a raised eyebrow when we might be too loud. A quiet scolding for asking too many questions. A change of subject when the conversation gets too heavy. Sometimes they're wrapped in good intentions: "Don't air our business," "Stay in a child's place," or "What happens in this house stays in this house." And often, silence is offered as protection, a way to shield ourselves and each other from a world that already misreads us, punishes us, and rarely holds space for our pain. It's about survival in systems built to break us. It's about preserving dignity when everything else feels stripped away. Over time, what was once meant to protect becomes a cage. We begin to quiet ourselves, not just in public and around strangers, but in private, in our own homes, our own mirrors, our own hearts. We become adept at masking our pain with smiles, using laughter as a shield, and supporting everyone else while neglecting our own needs. As a result, the silence deepens, not only in our surroundings but also within ourselves.

In communities still healing from the weight of historical trauma and systemic oppression, silence often walks hand in hand with pride. There is power in protecting the sacred, and beauty in choosing what to reveal and when. But when silence becomes the only language we know, we lose parts of ourselves. We begin to believe that feeling deeply is a weakness, that vulnerability is dangerous, and that healing is something we must do in private, if at all.

We forget our voices are lifelines, not liabilities. Truth-telling can be an act of insurrection. Breaking the silence does not disrespect those who came before us; instead, it liberates them. Our grandmothers, mothers, and aunties weren't wrong for staying silent; they were surviving. We get to do something they didn't always have: the space or permission to speak, heal, be soft, or be seen. Now, many of us are standing at the edge of a choice: continue to inherit silence or disrupt it. Do we keep wearing the mask or risk being seen? Should we continue editing ourselves to fit into someone else's comfort zone or speak in the fullness of who we are? This unlearning is not about blame; it's about restoration. It's about acknowledging that while silence got us here, it cannot take us where we're meant to go.

Emotion as a Threat

For many Black women, emotion has never been a neutral experience. It is studied, measured, and monitored, both by us and others. Our feelings are not simply felt; they are calculated. How will this be received? What will they assume about me? What will it cost me? Over time, emotional expression becomes less about honesty and more about safety. Not emotional safety, but physical, professional, and social survival.

We are rarely given the freedom to be emotionally full. From girlhood, we're taught to be careful with our tone, to soften our gaze, to monitor our body language. We are told, directly or through consequences, that certain feelings are not meant for public display. Sadness is perceived as fragility. Frustration becomes defiance. Grief is seen as indulgent. There is no cultural margin for our internal world to occupy. We become highly skilled at withholding, not because we lack emotion, but because we've been trained to protect ourselves from what feeling might cost us.

This conditioning doesn't just come from outside. Often, it's echoed in our own homes. Not from a place of harm, but from caution. We watched our mothers and aunties offer measured responses in moments that deserved raw emotion. We saw them show up to work, family events, and church gatherings, while hiding deep pain behind polished smiles and steady postures. We learned early what emotions were acceptable and which ones needed to be suppressed in silence. The ability to regulate our feelings became the mark of being "raised right," of appearing graceful under pressure, of staying calm even when something inside was unraveling.

The result is a subtle but profound separation from ourselves. We begin to second-guess what we feel. We filter even the most natural responses, wiping tears before they fall, minimizing joy in rooms that don't feel safe, withholding discomfort to keep the peace. Over time, our inner world grows quieter, not from lack of feeling but from lack of permission. This creates a dangerous illusion of control, one that leaves us disconnected from our own nervous systems. We feel tension without knowing its source. We carry fatigue that rest alone cannot cure. We walk around with full hearts and locked jaws, not realizing how much of our lives we've lived bracing for emotional consequences.

In this context, emotion is not only personal; it becomes political. There is an unspoken surveillance that follows us into professional spaces, classrooms, and even our most intimate relationships. If we advocate for ourselves, we're labeled combative. If we set a boundary, we're accused of being cold or distant. If we express confusion or hurt, we're seen as dramatic or unstable. The emotional double standard is relentless and exhausting. It forces us into performance, into perpetual curation of how we are perceived. We become fluent in emotional containment, fluent in reading the room before we know how to read ourselves.

This emotional tightrope isn't just stifling; it's unsustainable. Over time, it erodes our sense of self. When we are denied the space to feel fully, we are also denied the opportunity to heal. Healing requires truth and truth requires access to emotion. Without access, we become silent and numb rather than expressing our authenticity. It exhausts us in ways we struggle to articulate and slowly convinces us that feeling deeply is a flaw rather than a form of wisdom. However, the truth is our emotions are not liabilities. They are not evidence of failure or instability. They are sacred responses to our lived experience. Anger can signal injustice. Sadness can reveal where we need care. Longing can show us what matters. When we suppress these truths, we abandon ourselves. When we honor them, we find restoration.

Reclaiming emotional truth is a form of resistance, a quiet, embodied deliverance. It's sitting with what hurts instead of hiding it, naming what's real without apology. It's learning, perhaps for the first time, we don't need permission to feel, just the courage to belong to ourselves again.

The Disconnect Between Self and Emotion

There's an ache that doesn't show up in bruises or breaks but rather in the long pauses between questions like "How are you?" and the answer you want to give but don't. It reveals itself in the tight smile you offer when you're falling apart, the perfectly composed email you write with tears burning in your eyes. It's the weight of carrying feelings you've never been allowed to explore, because no one ever asked about them or modeled how to express them.

For numerous Black women, this emotional distance stems not from apathy but rather from a process of adaptation. We discover early on that those emotions – particularly the intense and complicated ones – can often be seen as liabilities. Vulnerability might not be met with care, but with punishment, mockery, or dismissal. So, we tucked our feelings away, not because we didn't feel deeply, but because we were afraid our feelings would be both too much for others and not enough for the people we needed most.

Over time, what begins as protection can transform into a prison. You may find yourself merely going through the motions – navigating career, family, and achievements – without truly engaging in your own life. Internally, you sense an increasing chasm between your inner self and your external existence. Doubts about your emotional instincts arise, as they were never cultivated; you may wonder if you're overreacting, overly sensitive, or too needy. You might even confuse suppression with strength. This internal disconnect isn't just confined to the mind; it manifests physically. You experience sleepless nights, a racing heart, and persistent muscle tension. Emotional detachment doesn't shield us from pain; rather, it buries it deeper. However, buried pain doesn't vanish—it festers, morphs, and eventually demands recognition. At times, it may present itself as chronic fatigue or unexplainable anxiety. Other times, it arrives as a quiet numbness, making you feel like a spectator in your own life.

We rarely discuss how emotional neglect, even when unintentional, can fracture our inner compass. How many of us reached adulthood without the words to say, "I'm not okay," without guilt or shame? No one handed us the tools for self-awareness or emotional literacy. We inherited responsibilities, roles, and expectations but not always the relational language needed to feel safe with ourselves. Healing is possible, and it begins with truth. Your emotions are not a burden; there's nothing wrong with you for struggling to connect to them, and you're not broken because you weren't taught how to feel. Relearning this begins with presence, stillness, and asking yourself the questions no one ever thought to ask you: *What do I need right now? What am I feeling underneath the numbness? Whose voice is telling me I can't rest, cry, feel, or soften?*

Emotional reparenting isn't just about caring for your inner child; it's about becoming the safe place you never had. It's about choosing, every day, to treat yourself with the tenderness, patience, and permission you once needed from someone else. It's not linear or tidy. Some days, you'll feel like you're moving backward. Some days, you'll catch yourself numbing again, saying you're "fine" when you're not. However, the difference is now noticeable. You'll pause. You'll gently come back to yourself.

This work isn't glamorous. It won't always appear to be a visible transformation. Sometimes it looks like taking a deep breath instead of brushing past your feelings. Sometimes it looks like choosing rest when your instinct is to push. Sometimes it's sitting in silence and letting the tears fall, not out of weakness but because you're finally safe enough to feel. You no longer have to perform for a world that refused to witness your humanity. You are the witness now.

Silence in Relationships

Silence also begins to quietly script how we relate to others. In relationships, silence becomes both a shield and a cage. It starts off as a means of protection, something that kept us safe in childhood, in hostile environments, in systems that never made space for our full humanity. Over time, the silence that once helped us survive begins to smother us. It bleeds into the way we love, communicate, connect, and grieve.

In romantic relationships, it manifests as an inability to ask for what we need without shame. It's the soft but constant refrain of *"I'm fine"* when we're anything but, biting our tongue during moments of hurt because we fear conflict will push them away. We second-guess ourselves before expressing discomfort. We replay conversations in our minds, wondering if we were too sensitive, too needy, too much. We worry speaking our truth will cause abandonment, or that our emotions will be dismissed, weaponized, or ridiculed. Instead, we say nothing and that silence builds. It settles into our bodies and takes up space in our chest. It becomes resentment without a voice, disappointment without air, and grief without a witness. When that emotional backlog becomes too much to hold, it erupts, not with intention, but with urgency. One moment, everything feels manageable; the next, we're crying over a missed phone call, lashing out over something small. It's not just about the dishes or the forgotten text, it's about everything we've been carrying quietly, invisibly, for months and sometimes years.

These outbursts often leave us feeling embarrassed, as if our own emotions have betrayed us. We may retreat, apologize excessively, or tell ourselves we're broken. We're not broken, we're burdened and exhausted. We've spent a lifetime trying to manage our inner world without bothering anyone, without making a mess, without being "too much." We've been trained to believe love requires silence, durability means emotional restraint, and vulnerability poses a risk we can't afford. So, in relationships, silence becomes a habit, a way of being, a language passed down like a curse.

It's not just romantic love where this shows up; it lives in our friendships and family dynamics too. We don't tell our closest friends when we're drowning. We keep secrets to avoid judgment. We stay quiet about betrayal or hurt until the friendship drifts into distance, and in our families, especially within Black love and generational bonds, silence is often mistaken for submission and femininity. We see women endure disappointment, betrayals, and abandonment, all without ever raising their voices. We're praised for being "low maintenance," "easygoing," "chill," but inside, we're aching to be seen and known.

Silence becomes our default, not because we have nothing to say, but because we've learned there may be consequences when we say it. We shrink by learned instinct, and eventually, emotional silence hardens into isolation. We're surrounded by people yet feel alone. We give and give but still feel unseen. We're physically present, but emotionally absent, even from ourselves. Underneath all of it is fear. Not just fear of losing others, but fear of what will rise to the surface if we tell the truth. Fear that once we open that door, we won't be able to close it. Fear that our pain, once spoken aloud, will make us unlovable. We let the silence remain until the silence begins to scream.

Breaking this cycle requires intention and tenderness. It means learning to voice our needs before they become emergencies, recognizing that asking for clarity, reassurance, or honesty simply makes us human. It means giving ourselves permission to be known, even when it feels risky. Perhaps most of all, it means realizing that love built on suppression is not sustainable. It may feel safe, but it will never be free.

Healing our relationship with conversation is one of the most radical things we can do for ourselves and those we love. It invites us to step out of emotional hiding, rewrite the script we were given, create relationships where truth is a bridge, not a threat, where our voice is cherished instead of tolerated. Where we don't have to choose between being loved and being honest. Love without voice is not love, it's performance. We are worthy of more than applause. We are worthy of intimacy, reciprocity, and the freedom to speak and be heard.

The Cost of Silence in Motherhood

The cost of silence in motherhood isn't always loud. It settles into the bones of our parenting, often unnoticed, until it begins to echo back through our children. Many Black women are mothering while still trying to piece together the parts of themselves they were never allowed to feel, to fall apart, or to fully be. We are trying to nurture when we were never fully nurtured, pouring from pitchers that were never filled.

We love our children fiercely. But fierce love, without emotional language or space to breathe, can still leave us emotionally hungry. We often overcompensate with structure, performance, survival strategies, doing everything right on paper while privately feeling numb, exhausted, or emotionally unreachable. We show up in all the ways we were taught mattered: discipline, responsibility, and excellence. But emotional presence wasn't modeled for many of us. We didn't grow up hearing "Tell me how you're really feeling." We weren't rocked through our meltdowns. We were told to hush, behave, and toughen up. So, we learned to do the same. But children don't just learn from what we say; they absorb how we live. They watch how we hold ourselves, how we react to stress, how we disappear into our responsibilities. When we're emotionally unavailable – not out of malice, but out of inherited silence – they feel it. Even if their bellies are full and the lights are on, they feel it. That quiet disconnection can lodge inside them like confusion: *Why can't I reach her? Why does love feel so far away?* This is how the wound passes on, not because we failed, but because we were never shown another way.

Sometimes, it breaks us to see our children start to silence themselves, too. When they stop coming to us. When their tears dry up too quickly. When their voices dim in our presence. We recognize something all too familiar in their withdrawal. That's when the ache becomes undeniable. We know that silence. We lived it. Silence doesn't have to be our legacy. We are allowed to begin again. Not as perfect mothers, but as whole human beings in progress. It starts with acknowledging parts of ourselves we still don't fully understand, parts grieving what we never received. That grief is sacred, not shameful. When we make space for our own emotional healing, we create an environment where our children can be fully seen.

More than any lesson or lecture, our children learn through witnessing. When they see us allow our tears to fall, they learn crying is not a sign of weakness. When they hear us name our feelings without guilt, they learn being overwhelmed doesn't mean we're incapable. They learn to express themselves when we stop silencing our own hearts, and they learn trust, not because we never make mistakes, but because we own them, repair them, and model tenderness through them. This is how we begin to parent differently: not from a place of perfection, but from a place of presence. From the decision to say what was never said. To listen without fixing. To validate without diminishing. To apologize when we miss the mark. To give ourselves compassion as we learn to be the mothers we needed, while still being the mothers our children deserve.

The cost of silence is steep, but the return of choosing to break it is immeasurable. When we choose to feel, we choose to love more deeply. When we speak, we invite connection. When we heal, we offer our children a new inheritance, one where love speaks, emotions flow, and silence no longer stands between us.

Reclaiming the Right to Feel

Reclaiming the right to feel is an act of rebellion. For Black women, emotional expression has too often been policed, punished, or pathologized. We've been conditioned to see our feelings as inconvenient, excessive, or dangerous. We were taught to hold them in, package them neatly, and hide beneath smiles or silence. But our emotions are not liabilities; they are evidence of our aliveness. They are sacred, valid, and necessary.

We come from lineages where survival demanded peace. Keeping things in was the only way to stay safe. But survival is not the same as wholeness. Many of us were never taught how to sit with grief, name loneliness, or feel joy without fearing it would be taken. We weren't given the language to say, "I'm hurt," without it being dismissed as an attitude. We weren't given the room to cry without being told we were too sensitive. So, we learned to tuck our feelings behind responsibility, achievement, and caretaking. We learned to survive by disconnecting from the very parts of ourselves that needed tending. But we're allowed to feel. We're allowed to break open and still be whole. Emotional expression is not a luxury; it is a release. Crying is not weakness. Softness is not fragility. Tenderness is not foolish. Rage is not a threat; it is a mirror, reflecting what has been harmed and what still longs to be heard. Our emotions are not burdens but rather bridges back to ourselves. For far too long, we've been told we must earn our right to feel by first proving our strength. But what if feeling is the strength? What if our ability to be with the fullness of our emotions, without shame or self-abandonment, is actually our greatest power?

When you've spent your life anticipating rejection, practicing emotional restraint, and managing other people's discomfort, letting yourself feel can feel radical. It can also feel terrifying, but that discomfort is not a sign to stop; it's a sign you're reclaiming space inside yourself. The body softens when it knows it's safe and we deserve safety, not just from the world, but within ourselves.

Reclaiming this right starts with presence. It's in the small, quiet acts, taking a breath before reacting. Sitting still long enough to notice what hurts beneath the anger. Journaling not just your accomplishments, but your fears, your questions, your longings. Writing the truth without needing to wrap it in politeness or pretty language. Some days, the words may come out jagged or unclear, but they are yours, and that matters. Somatic healing teaches us emotions are embodied. The tightness in your jaw, the tension in your shoulders, the ache behind your eyes that never entirely leaves: these are echoes of feelings you swallowed instead of speaking. Through breathwork, movement, and touch, we begin to unlearn the idea that we are not allowed to be at home in our own skin. We begin to offer ourselves the care we've longed for from others.

Storytelling can be another path to freedom. When we tell our stories, whether in a therapist's office, a group circle, or alone on the page, we stop performing and start existing. We stop editing ourselves for the sake of others' comfort. We say, "This happened, and I'm still here. This hurt, and I deserve healing. This is who I am, and I don't need to apologize for it." There is something holy in saying what was once unspeakable.

Therapy, too, can hold space for this reclamation. We deserve to be recognized in all our emotional complexity and humanity. A skilled therapist can help us untangle what we've been carrying for decades, things that don't even belong to us, passed down, never questioned, and those things we were too afraid to name. Therapy can offer permission and tools for building an emotional life we were never taught to create.

This isn't just about processing pain. It's also about reclaiming joy, letting yourself laugh out loud, or resting without guilt. Let yourself feel proud, loved, and hopeful without bracing for the fallout. Feeling deeply is how we know we're still here. It's how we connect to our intuition, creativity, softness, and rage. It's how we heal. Reclaiming the right to feel means no longer measuring our emotional expression against someone else's comfort. It means refusing to apologize for being human and holding space for each loud, soft, unsure, and fierce part of ourselves, knowing none of it makes us unworthy. In fact, it makes us free.

Creating Emotionally Safe Spaces

Emotionally safe spaces are not a given for Black women. They're fought for, built, and protected. Sometimes, they're imagined before they are ever fully lived. Many of us grew up without knowing what emotional safety feels like in our bodies. We may have known physical protection – ensuring we're fed, clothed, and unharmed – but emotional protection, the kind that allows you to break down without breaking apart, is often missing. We are praised for our strength but rarely offered softness in return. From a young age, many of us learned our feelings were liabilities, our tears made others uncomfortable, our anger made us dangerous, our joy made us targets. We learned to be "appropriate," monitoring tone, volume, and expression, survival skills masked as social intelligence, not because we lacked emotion, but because we were too aware of what happened when we expressed it. So, we quieted ourselves, even in spaces meant for us.

When I think about safe spaces, I think about those small, brief, sacred moments where we can just *be*. I've had those at work, where a glance or a side conversation with another Black woman became an anchor in the chaos. We exchanged knowing. In those moments, an invisible sanctuary formed between us. But even then, we were careful. We felt the stares if we lingered too long, heard the shift in tone when we took up space together. If more than two of us gathered at lunch, after a meeting, or during a walk down the hallway, it was *noticed*, and the message was clear: we are constantly being watched. These weren't just isolated experiences. They echoed something older, something systemic. The fear of Black unity. The legacy of controlling how, when, and where we come together. The trauma of slave patrols, being monitored on plantations, in public, in protests, in church, in life. That history lives in our nervous systems. We carry it in how we shrink, how we code-switch, how we become hyperaware of our presence. Even in joy, we brace. Even in laughter, we look around to see if we've become "too much."

This tension extends beyond professional spaces to families where love is shown, but feelings go unnamed, friendships where loyalty prevails but vulnerability is not always present, and communities where survival has required silence and breaking that silence feels like betrayal. We crave spaces where we can be held in our full humanity, not just our labor, not just our leadership, not just our performance of "having it all together," but in our sorrow, softness, confusion, and happiness. We don't always trust we can have that, let alone deserve it, so we build it, slowly and imperfectly. We learn how to ask better questions in our friendships. We risk crying in front of someone we love. We practice saying, "I'm not okay," without rushing to make others comfortable. We find therapists who look like us, who don't flinch when we speak our truth. We join sister circles where our voice becomes sacred, not shameful. We start creating emotional homes where we feel safe enough to unravel and strong enough to rebuild.

We turn inward, too. Sometimes the most dangerous judgment doesn't come from outside but rather lives within. We silence ourselves before anyone else can. We second-guess our emotions, dismiss our pain, and punish our tenderness. Learning to be emotionally safe with ourselves, *to stop hiding from our own feelings,* is the hardest, most necessary work. It means choosing not to abandon ourselves as others may have. It means saying, "This sadness belongs. This anger has a voice. This joy is mine to feel."

Emotionally safe spaces are more than rooms or relationships: they're acts of boldness. They are where we undo the damage of generations who had no choice but to suppress and survive, where we finally breathe without holding back. They are where our tears don't need explanation, our rage doesn't need apology, and our joy doesn't need to be dimmed.

We are not too much. We are not too loud, too sensitive, too complicated. We are whole, and we deserve spaces that honor that wholeness. Let this serve as a reminder that we can create the safe space we desire. Our emotions are not a burden; rather, they act as a guide for our journey of self-discovery.

Think about the silence you inherited, the things never spoken aloud but lived heavy in the air. What did that silence teach you about love, pain, or belonging? Ask yourself how silence shaped your voice: did it quiet it? Sharpen it? And now, as you come into deeper self-awareness, what truths are asking to be said, even if your voice trembles? There is no rush, but there is now an opportunity to speak.

Chapter 3
LOVE IN A WAR ZONE

"How can I let love in when I've spent my whole life building walls to stay alive?"

Love should feel like home. For many of us, love has often felt like a battlefield. We enter relationships carrying wounds never ours to bear, passed down through generations, born from abandonment, systemic dehumanization, and a culture that rarely mirrors back our softness. We are taught to be strong, to hold others down, to sacrifice our needs for the survival of our people. So, when love comes, we don't always know how to receive it – especially if it doesn't look like a struggle.

For so long, I believed love had to be hard. That love meant endurance. That it required me to constantly prove myself, through silence, sacrifice, and staying even when everything in me longed to leave. I thought love looked like holding on no matter the cost, and loyalty meant accepting less than I deserved. I had been taught, consciously and unconsciously, being chosen meant contorting myself, dimming my light, and giving more than I had, just to be worthy of someone's affection. It wasn't love; it was survival masquerading as devotion. I had to learn love isn't supposed to hurt. It isn't earned through suffering. Loyalty should not be confused with self-abandonment. Before I could learn what love really is, I had to unlearn everything I'd been taught about who I needed to be to deserve it. That unlearning didn't happen all at once. It happened in pieces, through heartbreak, through loneliness, through the painful realization I had been calling harm "home" for far too long. It meant sitting with the ache of my own unmet needs and finally asking why I'd made so much room for everyone else's. It meant grieving the little girl in me who thought being good, quiet, helpful, or low maintenance would be enough to make someone stay. I had to see the truth in the patterns I had normalized, how often I mistook chaos for chemistry, silence for peace, and scarcity for love. I had to be honest about how many times I gave away parts of myself in the hope someone would see me, choose me, and make it all worth it.

I come from a lineage of women who loved through pain, endured in silence, and believed staying, no matter how much it hurt, was the measure of their strength. While I honor the sacrifice and survival that brought me here, I refuse to inherit suffering as my standard. I want more. I deserve more. I am learning now real love is not built on pain. Real love is steady, tender. It listens without judgment and holds without trying to fix. It welcomes your wholeness, your softness, your anger, your dreams, your fears, without asking you to shrink or silence yourself. Real love feels like fuel, not exhaustion. It allows you to rest. To be. To bloom without apology. And perhaps most importantly, I am learning the first love I must reclaim is the love I give to myself. If I do not believe I am worthy of ease, I will continue to invite struggle. If I do not learn how to treat myself with gentleness, I will continue to accept harm and call it passion. I must become the sanctuary I've been searching for in others.

Love in a war zone is all many of us have ever known. But we are allowed to want more than survival. We are allowed to long for softness, to demand reciprocity, to be held with care. We are allowed to rewrite the story. We are allowed to heal. The kind of love we deserve doesn't hurt, doesn't deplete, and doesn't ask us to prove our worth. It reminds us, again and again, we are already enough. We are no longer auditioning for belonging. We are becoming the love we've always needed.

Lessons in Loneliness

Growing up, I saw Black women love hard. I saw them stay. I saw them fight for families, for partners, for sons and daughters, and husbands who never truly saw the weight they carried. I saw women pour into others until they were empty, then rise the next day and do it again. I watched their love stretch across impossible circumstances, their devotion stitched together with grit and sacrifice. There was beauty in their strength, but also quiet sorrow in how little room they had to fall apart. That was the model I inherited. That was the language I learned.

As a result, I learned early: to love someone meant to sacrifice, to endure, to prove yourself over and over again. I believed love was transactional, something to fight for, something that lived on the other side of suffering. And when I found myself in relationships, I followed that blueprint without question. I poured and poured, thinking if I just loved enough, held it together long enough, forgave enough, then maybe I could be chosen. I could be safe. I could matter.

Choosing someone else over yourself isn't love. It's fear, and fear was the foundation of so many of my relationships: fear of abandonment, fear of being alone, fear I would never be enough to make someone stay. Fear I would always be too much or not quite enough. My sensitivity was a liability. My truth would push people away. I didn't know then that love rooted in fear will always leave you empty. I thought that if I was needed, I'd be loved. If I could be indispensable, I'd be irreplaceable. But being needed is not the same as being cherished. And surviving love is not the same as being nurtured by it.

I confused passion with pain. I confused emotional chaos with chemistry. I thought the highs and lows meant depth, that the unpredictability meant intensity. I mistook struggle for sincerity and silence for peace. I built entire homes for people who only ever offered me shelter when it was convenient for them. Each time I was left behind, I blamed myself, thinking if I had just been more, done more, said less, smiled better, given more grace, then maybe I would have been enough to stay.

Loneliness has its lessons. It teaches you the difference between attachment and love, as well as the distinction between validation and worth. It teaches you how to sit with yourself, how to soothe the ache without trying to fill it with someone else. It reveals the places where you've abandoned yourself while trying so hard not to be abandoned by others. And in that quiet, that stillness, you begin to hear something softer – your own voice and needs, your own desire to come home to yourself.

I'm still unlearning. Still healing. But I know now that love does not demand your disappearance. You don't have to fracture yourself to be worthy of belonging. Loneliness isn't proof of failure;

sometimes it's a sacred pause, a doorway to deeper self-love. And maybe, just maybe, the loneliness was never about not being chosen by others. Maybe it was about finally choosing me.

The Walls We Build

Black women are often shamed for being guarded but no one talks about why. No one asks where the walls came from, who built them, and what we were trying to survive. We're not born cold. We're not naturally distant or difficult to love. We become guarded because the world teaches us, over and over, that being too open makes us a target. That sharing too much can be used against us. Showing softness without armor can cost us our dignity, our safety, even our sense of self. Vulnerability, for us, doesn't always feel like a bridge to connection; it often feels like a risk we cannot afford to take.

We are taught, whether by family, society, or experience, love must be earned through service, struggle, or quietness. We become fluent in the language of self-protection, learn to love from a distance, even while standing next to someone. We perfect the art of emotional multitasking, showing up for others while hiding parts of ourselves. We give just enough to feel close but never enough to feel exposed. Not because we don't want to be known, but because we've been shown that being fully known is not always safe. We become the resilient ones. The ones who hold it all together. And underneath all that strength? There's often a quiet, unspoken grief for the times we needed someone to keep us, but instead had to hold ourselves.

I remember one relationship where I was deeply in love – or so I believed. He said all the right things. He knew my trauma. He listened intently when I spoke about my childhood, my fears, and my dreams. He looked at me like he saw me. I wanted so badly to believe he did. Somewhere along the way, he started using my vulnerability as leverage. My softness became a liability in his eyes, something to manipulate, something to disarm. My strength wasn't honored; it became something he tried to break down, control, and dominate. And my loyalty? That was expected, not reciprocated. Still, I stayed. Not because I lacked awareness but because I still thought love was supposed to feel like a survival instinct. Like struggle. Like sacrifice.

I stayed longer than I should have. Deep within, I believed that love must be a struggle to be genuine. I thought that by giving more, being more tolerant, and forgiving more, it would eventually transform into the love I truly desired. That eventually, my worthiness would be proven. That pain was the price of being chosen. But leaving him wasn't just about walking away from a man. It was about walking away from a narrative that had lived in my bones for far too long, one that told me love should cost me everything. That being loved meant being needed, even if I was being drained in the process. That devotion meant self-abandonment, boundaries made me difficult, and silence made me safe.

Walking away meant confronting the version of myself confusing chaos with chemistry, control with care, and suffering with significance. It meant standing in front of the mirror and seeing not a failure, but a woman who had done the best she could with what she had, finally ready to believe she didn't have to bleed for connection, to carry the entire emotional load to be seen as worthy of love.

The walls we build are not random. They are carefully crafted through years of trying to remain whole in a world that constantly asks us to fracture ourselves. They are made of heartbreak and high alert, of expectations never met and needs never named. However, those walls, which once kept us safe, can eventually become prisons. They keep the pain out, yes, but they also keep the love out. The softness. The warmth. The joy.

Now, I am slowly learning safety and love can co-exist. I don't have to choose between protecting myself and being open. I can set boundaries and still be soft. I can be guarded when I need to but don't have to live behind the wall forever. Real love, the kind that heals instead of harms, will never ask me to trade in my dignity for affection. It will never weaponize my wounds or twist my truth. It will sit with me in the mess and still choose me, not in spite of my complexity, but because of it. And maybe the bravest thing I've ever done is not just leaving the pain, but believing I deserve something gentler. Believing I am worthy of a love that feels like peace, home, and freedom. Believing I can slowly, brick by brick, build something new, not walls this time, but bridges that lead me back to myself. Back to trust. Back to love that doesn't hurt.

Deserving Better

Part of healing is realizing you are worthy of love that doesn't demand your suffering, test your loyalty through hardship, or measure your value by how much you're willing to lose yourself. Love should feel like clarity, not confusion. It stands firm, even when life is messy. And most importantly, love starts with you. It's the way you speak to yourself in your own mind. The boundaries you set without guilt. The joy you allow yourself to feel without apology. Self-love isn't a performance; it's a quiet, grounded decision to honor yourself. It's waking up and remembering your needs matter, not just in theory, but in practice. It's learning to say no without explanation and yes without fear. It's recognizing that your intuition is not something to second-guess, but something to trust deeply, especially in love.

Self-love is about holding space for your own sadness without rushing to fix it. It's how you advocate for your peace, even when others don't understand your silence. It's turning inward with compassion instead of criticism. It's taking the time to nourish the parts of you the world never bothered to see: your softness, your sensitivity, your stillness. The more I practiced self-love, the more I understood wholeness wasn't something I needed to earn. It was already mine. I just had to stop outsourcing my worth to people who couldn't hold it.

Now, I no longer wait to be chosen. I choose myself every single time. With that choice comes a deeper level of discernment. I pay attention to how people make me feel in their presence, whether I expand or contract, whether I feel safe or on edge. I don't chase potential anymore. I don't entertain people who admire my light but aren't willing to stand in the truth of it. I don't confuse proximity with connection. I know now alignment is not about intensity, it's about ease. Peace isn't passive, it's powerful. And I've learned real love doesn't ask me to become someone else. It meets me as I am. It evolves with me, growing in tandem with my growth.

I used to think letting go meant failure. Healing has taught me that releasing what doesn't serve me is one of the highest acts of love I can give myself. I no longer hold onto people just because we have history. I've stopped making homes out of temporary hearts. Now, I build sanctuary within. I've learned solitude can be sacred: not something to fear but to cherish. In the stillness, I hear my own voice clearly. I hear the version of me no longer begging to be seen but simply resting in the truth that I am already enough.

I no longer dim my light to make others comfortable. I shine. If it blinds the wrong ones, they were never for me. My softness is not a weakness. My boundaries are bridges to safety. I don't need to be everything to everyone. I just need to be whole to myself. In that wholeness, I find freedom that says *I am not too much. I am not too sensitive. I am not too bold. I am exactly who I need to be.* I am deserving – not someday, not when I'm perfect, but right now. As I am. I have finally come to understand I am not hard to love, I am just no longer available for anything or anyone unworthy of me.

A New Kind of Love

There is a love available to you that is soft, sacred, and steady. It does not come to break you. It comes to mirror the love you've been cultivating within. But to experience that kind of love, you must first lay down your weapons. The same armor that kept you safe is the armor that keeps love out. You were not made for battle every day. You were made for bliss, for ease, for arms that hold, not hurt you. You deserve to be seen and held in the fullness of your light and your wounds, your brilliance and your fears. You deserve love that feels like home, not a war zone.

I didn't always believe that. I once found myself in a relationship with someone who demanded to be the center of my world, as if my life and my children's well-being should orbit around his needs. Every conversation became a negotiation for my autonomy. He grew resentful whenever I made a decision that prioritized my children or even my own long-term dreams. He wanted control masked as commitment. We would constantly argue over everything, from how I spent my time to the tone of my voice. He questioned my choices as a mother, as a woman, as a human being. He made it clear that unless he came first, he would punish me with silence, outbursts, or cruel words meant to cut me down.

The verbal abuse didn't always come loudly. Sometimes it was the sigh when I said I had a busy day with the kids. Sometimes it was the subtle digs at my independence, or the mocking way he'd call me "too much" when I dared to express my needs. Other times, it was a full-blown eruption, marked by name-calling, shouting, and shaming me for not making him my priority. And for a while, I questioned myself. I wondered if maybe I was asking for too much. I wondered if I could make it work if I just adjusted a little more, bent a little further, dimmed just enough to keep the peace. But peace doesn't come from pretending. It doesn't grow in places you're not allowed to be whole. The day I finally let him go wasn't loud. It was quiet, precise, and necessary. I looked at my children and knew I couldn't teach them about love while being in a relationship with control and conditional acceptance. I knew love should never ask me to choose between my dignity and devotion. Releasing him felt like exhaling for the first time in years. I didn't just reclaim my time; I reclaimed my truth and made space for the kind of love that honors my motherhood, my voice, and my vision.

I know better now. I know love doesn't demand my silence or my sacrifice. It doesn't ask me to disappear inside someone else's shadow. It meets me in the light, stands beside me in partnership, and respects the totality of who I am. That is the kind of love I welcome now. And that is the kind of love I give to myself, daily, fiercely, and without apology.

Explore the difference between being loved and being

needed. Have you ever equated sacrifice with safety? Has

survival distorted your understanding of intimacy? Reflect

on how you show up in relationships when your nervous

system is still holding past alarms. What would love feel like

without the fear of loss, betrayal, or abandonment? Imagine

love that doesn't require your exhaustion.

Chapter 4
BEYOND THE BLAME

There is a quiet ache sitting between Black men and women, a growing tension that too often goes unnamed but never unfelt. It shows up in our conversations and in the way we flinch at one another's wounds. It's an ache rooted in generations of shared trauma, systemic racism, family separation, mass incarceration, and economic disenfranchisement. And yet instead of drawing us closer, those traumas often wedge us apart. We've both been wounded by the same systems, but still turn that pain toward each other.

I've felt it in my own relationships. The subtle mistrust, the unspoken expectations, the way love starts out tender and slowly becomes guarded. The need to be seen battling with the need to be safe. I've heard Black men speak of feeling unloved or unappreciated, while my sisters and I have felt unseen, unsupported, or emotionally abandoned. It's not always malicious. Sometimes, it's simply because we were never taught how to love each other through our pain. We were taught survival. We were taught to endure. But intimacy, vulnerability, and emotional safety? Those weren't part of the curriculum.

Patriarchy and racism both distort what love looks like between us. Patriarchy tells men they must dominate or suppress their emotions to be worthy. Racism and sexism forces women to be strong and self-reliant to survive. We come together armored, guarded, and exhausted. We meet each other with masks instead of open hearts. When love fails, we point fingers. Really, so much of the fracture lives beneath the surface, buried under layers of inherited pain.

We often hear "Black love is revolutionary," and it is, but only when it's built on truth, not performance. That truth includes the betrayal, the abandonment, the emotional unavailability many of us have experienced. It also includes the deep, persistent longing to be loved without having to earn it through pain, without shrinking, without constantly proving our worth.

The work of healing begins when we dare to look beyond the blame, pause the narrative of who hurt who first, and begin to ask, *'Where does it hurt?'* What if we stopped trying to win the pain Olympics and made room for each other's truth? That doesn't mean tolerating harm or bypassing accountability; it means being brave enough to see the human underneath the defense mechanisms.

I want softness between us again. I want mutual respect and emotional safety. I want us to be allowed to be flawed and still worthy of love. To not confuse silence with peace. To not confuse struggle with loyalty. To not confuse distance with protection. We deserve more than recycled trauma masquerading as love.

For Black women especially, it's time to stop contorting ourselves to be palatable, to be chosen, to be enough. We are already enough. For Black men, it's time to be seen in your full emotional truth, not just as protectors or providers, but as whole, feeling beings. This healing must be collective. We need each other. But first, we must face the silence, resentment, fragility, and fear with courage. Beyond the blame is the possibility of rebuilding, of loving again but on our own terms with tenderness, grace, and truth.

The Wound Between Us

There is a wound between us that lives in our glances, our guardedness, our silences. One that pulses even when we don't speak it aloud. It's historical, ancestral, systemic. It's what happens when people have been separated not just by physical distance but by centuries of psychological warfare. The wound between Black men and Black women is not merely the result of failed relationships, it is the inheritance of forced disconnection, of survival shaped in isolation.

Slavery didn't just strip us of names and land. It stripped us of the right to belong to one another fully. To raise our children in safety. To protect each other in peace. It dismantled trust before we had a chance to build it. Even as time passed, the mechanisms of separation persisted. We were taught, both subtly and violently, that love between us was dangerous, impractical, or doomed.

So we grieve but often, we don't know where to place that grief. Instead of being held and honored, it gets directed sideways towards each other. Our shared trauma begins to look like personal betrayal. Our unmet needs become accusations. Our pain, unprocessed, sharpens into blame. It's not because we don't love each other but because we've been taught love must be earned by overcoming challenges and enduring hardships.

We've been conditioned to mistrust the very people who look like us. We internalized roles, provider, protector, strong Black woman, emotionally unavailable Black man, without ever being shown how to be fully human with one another.

There is so much longing underneath the ache. Longing to be chosen, to feel safe in each other's arms, but the world has made it hard to know what safety even looks like. We've spent so long surviving that intimacy feels foreign, something we want but don't know how to receive without fearing loss or betrayal.

This wound isn't just about romantic relationships; it also affects friendships, families, and community spaces. It shows up when we don't believe each other's pain, when we dismiss each other's vulnerability, when we project our hurt instead of naming it, when we forget we both carry the same weight, just hold it in different ways. We keep missing each other, not because we don't care, but because our pain sometimes speaks louder than our love.

The presence of the wound doesn't mean we're beyond repair. It reveals how deeply we still desire connection. That desire is sacred. It means there is still something worth tending to. We don't need to pretend the harm never happened or that we know exactly how to heal it, but we can begin by telling the truth about what's been lost, what still hurts, and what we never learned how to ask for. We can start by not seeing each other as threats but as mirrors, wounded, yes, but still worthy of care.

Healing this wound is not about rushing back into each other's arms. It's about slowing down long enough to understand what created the distance in the first place, grieving the love we never got to give fully, and choosing to see each other through the eyes of compassion, even when it's hard. Especially when it's hard.

We are not broken. We are grieving, and underneath that grief is the possibility of something tender. Not perfect, but honest and real. Something rooted in mutual care, not codependency. Something that allows us to show up in our fullness, not just in our function. Something that doesn't demand we shrink or harden to belong.

This is our work: not just to love each other but to unlearn the reasons we stopped trusting love in the first place. To reclaim a kind of intimacy that isn't built on power, pain, or performance but on presence, truth, and mutual liberation. Let us not be afraid to name the wound, because in naming it, we begin the process of healing together.

Armor Meets Armor

When armor meets armor, love doesn't flow. It ricochets. Words are heard but not felt. Intentions are buried under interpretation. And two people who need each other deeply end up standing on opposite shores, both convinced the other is unreachable. But it's not because we don't care. It's because we've been taught care is dangerous when not filtered through control.

Patriarchy didn't skip over us. Racism didn't spare our relationships. They both crept in and settled between us, convincing us to brace rather than soften. As Black women, we've been taught we must always be ten steps ahead, strong, composed, and unbothered. We were handed resilience before we were offered rest. We learned to do everything, from raising children, to earning degrees, to holding families and communities, without flinching, because flinching made us vulnerable and we learned vulnerability was a luxury we could not afford.

Black men, our mirrors, our kin, were not spared either. Stripped of the space to be tender, they were taught emotions should be locked away, that softness made them targets and the only acceptable forms of expression were anger or silence. They were policed in their feelings just as violently as they were policed in the streets. Their humanity was not nurtured. And so they, too, learned to lead with armor.

When we come together, both carrying years, lifetimes, generations of learned defense, something tender within us gets lost in translation. We show up guarded and mistake each other's shields for swords. A woman who protects her peace is often labeled bitter. A man masking his hurt is called cold. Neither is fully seen, only the surface-level projections of what pain has shaped us into.

I know this dynamic too intimately: the emotional hesitancy, the disconnect with no apparent cause, the quiet ache of knowing someone is close but not available. I've tried to love through a wall, tried to be understood while hiding my own need to be held. I've watched as the weight of someone else's silence mirrored my own. In those moments, it wasn't that we didn't care. We didn't know how to let each other in.

This is the wound we rarely name. We're more experienced in self-protection than in intimacy, more fluent in proving ourselves than in revealing ourselves. And when we live in a world constantly telling us we're not safe, that makes a tragic kind of sense. But if we want something different, something sacred, we have to move differently. The first step is to unlearn the idea that being unbreakable is the ultimate goal. Being emotionally alive, being honest, being soft enough to feel and strong enough to name what you need – that's what real power looks like and where real connection lives.

Imagine a world where Black men could cry without shame, where they didn't have to choose between love and masculinity, where they weren't taught expressing pain made them weak. Imagine a world where Black women didn't have to qualify their softness, didn't have to be the safe space and the savior at the same time. Where they could say "I need help" without being met with guilt or silence. We're not there yet but we can begin in our own lives, in our own relationships. We can start by acknowledging when our fear speaks louder than our hearts. We can begin by asking ourselves: *Is this reaction about the person in front of me, or is it about who hurt me before?* We can start by softening where it feels safe to do so and creating boundaries where it doesn't.

Armor has its place. It protected us when nothing else could, but protection is not the same as connection. One keeps people out. The other invites people in. And we deserve connection. We deserve to be witnessed fully and loved deeply, not in spite of our wounds but with a complete understanding of them. This is not about blame. It's about awareness. It's about understanding we have inherited wounds but we don't have to pass them on. The stories we were given about who we had to be in love, stoic, invulnerable, impenetrable, were never the whole story. We are allowed to want more than survival, to enjoy intimacy honoring our wholeness. We are allowed to put the armor down, not all at once, not recklessly, but in places where love is ready to meet us. Where we are no longer asked to shrink or shield, but simply to *be*. When that day comes, when two people meet not through armor but through clarity, courage, and care, something generational begins to shift. The silence breaks, the mistrust softens, and a real, rooted connection becomes possible again.

Emotional Currency: What We Trade for Love

There is a quiet cost Black women often carry in relationships, a cost we've been taught not to question. We give time, energy, care, and presence, often without being asked, because we were raised to believe love means being available. Being accommodating. Being steady, even when we're unraveling inside. Somewhere along the way, we were taught showing up for others was a sign of value. So, we overextend.

We manage feelings, keep the peace, take on the weight of others' needs before even considering our own. Over time, we learn to go without. Not because we don't want love in return, but because we're used to being the ones who hold things together.

This is the kind of emotional labor that becomes invisible until it drains us. It's not the kind that gets acknowledged or celebrated. It's the kind people expect without realizing the impact. We say we're okay when we're not. We stay quiet to avoid conflict or overreact because we haven't been taught to transmute our energy. We give more because we don't want to be seen as demanding and in doing so, we often end up alone, even while in partnership.

On the other side, many Black men are socialized into a different kind of silence. They're discouraged from speaking from the heart or checking in with their emotions. They're told to be dependable, to provide, and to protect without the space to practice emotional closeness. Love, then, becomes about what they can do, not how they can be. It's measured by presence, responsibility, and action rather than emotional availability.

This creates a disconnect, two people who care for each other but don't reach each other. Both people seek connection but feel depleted in different ways. The woman may feel taken for granted. The man may feel unappreciated. No one wins, yet both feel they're giving everything they can.

What makes this dynamic even more painful is that the effort on both sides is real. The Black woman who feels unseen often gives more than she has to offer. The Black man who feels misunderstood often loves in the only way he has been shown. These are not careless people. They are people doing their best within a system that hasn't taught them how to connect emotionally.

Over time, the absence of emotional fulfillment can turn into quiet resentment. Communication becomes limited. Affection becomes inconsistent. There is no longer space to be vulnerable because neither person feels safe enough to open up. Misunderstanding becomes the norm, not the exception.

We are not broken. But we have inherited broken frameworks for how to love and be loved. When emotional needs are never understood, they cannot be met. When care is given without boundaries, it can become a form of self-neglect. When we are praised for being "strong" or "responsible," but not nurtured in our emotional lives, we lose connection, not just with others, but with ourselves.

It's time to create new agreements built on mutual understanding and respect, rather than on guilt or expectation. Relationships don't thrive on one person giving endlessly and the other person guessing what's wrong. They thrive with emotional clarity when both people can say, "This is what I need," "This is how I feel," and "This is what I can offer."

Loving someone doesn't mean neglecting yourself. Being present for someone doesn't mean shutting down your emotions. We don't have to choose between connection and well-being; genuine relationships allow for both. This is not about blame. It's about awareness. We're allowed to want emotional care that feels balanced, to ask for presence that isn't just physical, but also emotional. We're allowed to be honest about how we feel without fear of being dismissed.

We have been conditioned to adapt, accept the bare minimum and lower our standards so we don't feel like we're asking too much, but emotional care is not a luxury. It's a need. If we are to move forward in love – not just romantic, but communal and personal – we must be willing to tell the truth about what we've given, what we've lost, and what we still long for.

You don't have to trade your well-being for closeness. You don't have to carry someone's emotions while dismissing your own, and you don't have to settle for relationships where care only moves in one direction. You can start naming your needs. Stop overextending. Ask to be considered in the same ways you consider others. That is not selfishness. That is self-honoring, and from that place, we can build something new, relationships rooted not in imbalance, but in care that moves both ways.

Relearning Love

Relearning love is not a return but rather an initiation into something many of us were never given. It's about moving from inherited patterns to intentional choices. For Black couples, it's an act of resistance and renewal. It begins with the willingness to see our relationships as spaces where healing is both welcomed and expected, rather than as extensions of our wounds. With that shift, that quiet turning inward, everything changes.

So many of us were taught love means showing up even when we're empty, staying quiet so the peace isn't disturbed. It seems that endurance, even when we're breaking inside, is what we've known; if that's all we've known, it makes sense love has felt like pressure. However, love that requires us to sacrifice our true selves is not genuine love; it is merely survival disguised as connection.

To relearn love is to unfasten ourselves from those expectations. To stop performing closeness and instead create it from the inside out. It's choosing to meet each other not with assumptions but with understanding. It's sitting in the discomfort of honesty and choosing to stay anyway, not because we are afraid to lose each other but because we are learning how to hold each other with care.

For Black men and women, this requires a deliberate shift away from the roles we've been assigned. Black men are often socialized to equate love with providing and protecting, but not necessarily with being emotionally available. Black women are taught love is sacrifice and care means carrying it all. Together, these beliefs form a dynamic rewarding performance but that starves emotional connection. One gives what they were taught they had to; the other accepts what they've been conditioned to expect.

Beneath all of that is a longing to be seen, known, and loved not for what we do but for who we are. Relearning love asks us to meet that longing directly. It asks us to move past duty and toward mutuality. To replace roles with relationships. To create room for nuance and imperfection, and to be willing to grow alongside one another, even when it's uncomfortable.

This isn't about swapping one dynamic for another. It's about building something that feels real. Something that honors the full spectrum of what it means to be in partnership: tenderness, conflict, accountability, and grace. Intimacy is not built in grand gestures; it's built in the consistency of emotional presence. It's being willing to say: "I'm hurt," or "I'm scared," or "I need you to meet me here," and trusting that you won't be met with punishment or distance.

That kind of love doesn't happen by default. It happens by choice. It's in the small acts of listening without defending. In the courage to apologize without being coerced. The ability to ask for what you need without shame. It's in the capacity to receive love when it's offered, without bracing for it to be taken away.

For us to move forward, we need new relationship models that center dignity and softness rather than power or control. Relationships where both people can breathe, speak, and rest. Where mutual respect is the standard, not the exception. Where we hold one another accountable without stripping each other of humanity. Where we don't confuse emotional labor with love or silence with strength.

We relearn love one moment at a time. A conversation that doesn't end in shutdown. A boundary that is respected instead of ignored. An act of care that isn't used as leverage. It doesn't have to be dramatic or loud. It just has to be true.

In that truth, we get to become something different than what we saw growing up. Something more whole, more generous, more honest. Something that honors our complexity, rather than punishes it. Something that feels like home, not because we never disagree, but because we can disagree without destroying each other.

You don't have to choose between intimacy and authenticity. You don't have to sacrifice your voice to be held, and you don't have to prove your worth to receive care. Relearning love is a journey back to emotional safety. And from that place, we don't just stay, we thrive.

The Collective Healing

The healing between us is not just about romantic reconciliation; it's about reclaiming something bigger than ourselves. Black love, in all its forms, is an act of remembering. Remembering that we are not enemies, that the divide between us was never of our making. Despite what we've been told and what we've endured, we are still each other's home.

Black love is not limited to partnership. It's how we show up in community, how we raise our children, how we speak to one another in the grocery store, in the hallway, in the quiet spaces where no one is watching. It's the energy we pass between brothers and sisters, between elders and youth, between chosen family and kin. It is the softness in our presence, the truth in our language, the care we extend even when we're tired. And this love, communal, ancestral, defiant, is the foundation of our collective freedom.

To repair the rift between Black men and women, we must first acknowledge its existence. We didn't fail but we *were* wounded. Systems of oppression have targeted our unity, forcing us into roles rupturing our connection. But we don't have to stay divided. Healing this rift is not about returning to a version of us that never really existed; it's about co-creating something new. Something honest. Something grounded in shared care, not shared pain.

This kind of healing requires more than dialogue. It requires courage. The courage to see beyond our own hurt and make room for each other's humanity, to stop demanding perfection before offering love, to stop holding one another hostage to roles we didn't choose. It asks us to move slowly, with intention, and to extend the grace we've all been desperate to receive. We can't wait until we are completely healed to show up for one another. That day may never come. However, we can choose to love while we heal. To care while growing. To forgive while learning.

Love cannot survive under the weight of conditional acceptance. We cannot continue to demand suffering as proof of devotion. We don't need to earn love through pain, endurance, or self-denial. We are worthy now as we are. Flawed, growing, imperfect, and still deeply deserving.

Collective healing is not about fixing each other. It's about holding space for each other to be fully human. To be heard, seen, and met with care, even when we don't have the right words. It's about honoring that our healing is intertwined. When we turn toward each other instead of away, we create something powerful. Something unshakable. We don't have to agree on everything to be in community; we have to agree to keep showing up. To keep choosing softness when defensiveness wants to take over. To keep in mind the enemy is not each other. It never was.

Our liberation depends on our ability to love without conditions. To see one another beyond survival roles and root into something deeper, something that lives beyond performance and pain.

Something that reminds us we are still here, still loving, still worthy of beginning again. This is the work, and we are deserving of it.

77

Take a moment to reflect on the ways you've experienced or

witnessed the ache between Black men and women, the

unspoken distance, the defensiveness, the longing

underneath the silence. When have you felt unseen,

misunderstood, or guarded in your relationships? When have

you unintentionally met someone else's pain with your own

armor?

Explore the stories you've carried about who's at fault or

who should have shown up differently. What shifts when

you stop asking *who's to blame* and begin asking *what was*

hurting? Where in your life is there space for repair, without needing to be right, without needing to win, just with the courage to tell the truth?

Let this be an invitation to grieve what was missing and to imagine what becomes possible when love is no longer shaped by survival. What does softness, truth, and emotional safety look like for you now, in your relationships, in your community, and within yourself?

Chapter 5
CORPORATE CHAMELEON

"I had to wear a mask to earn a seat at the table. But once I got there, I realized the table was never built for me, but I claimed my seat anyway."

For many of us, success was the escape plan. We were told that if we got the degrees, spoke the language, dressed the part, and climbed the ladder, we would finally be safe. Respected. Seen. So, we played the game. We changed our hair. We adjusted our tone. We became palatable. We code-switched our way into rooms our ancestors could only dream of but once we arrived, we realized we were still fighting for permission to exist. The closer we got to "making it," the further we felt from ourselves. This chapter is about that distance. The quiet disconnection that grows when you trade authenticity for acceptance.

The emotional exhaustion of carrying everyone else's comfort while abandoning your own. The silent grief of becoming a stranger to yourself in exchange for a paycheck, a title, or a seat at the table.

I lived that grief. Day after day, I showed up, tucked away in a version of myself that fit the mold. My real thoughts, my real feelings, my real voice, locked inside a box I thought I had to live in to survive. I wore the mask so well it became second skin. I smiled when I wanted to scream. I nodded in agreement to ideas that left my spirit unsettled. I overachieved, overextended, and overdelivered to feel like I had earned my space. Every morning, I stood in front of the mirror preparing the look for the role I'd perfected: polished, pleasant, professional. But behind my eyes was a woman exhausted from hiding. I was surviving, yes, but I was also slowly vanishing.

Then came the moment that cracked everything open. I was sitting at a leadership table, surrounded by high rank and protocol, when, across from me, sat a Black woman who radiated something I hadn't seen in that space before: it was freedom. She was a full-bird colonel in the United States Air Force. A woman who had climbed the ranks, not by erasing herself but by standing firmly in her truth. Her presence was commanding. She carried herself with unapologetic ease. She didn't demand attention. She didn't code-switch. She didn't perform. She didn't shrink to fit the room. She *was* the room. Watching her was like watching the future I had forgotten was possible.

I couldn't stop thinking about her. The image of her sitting there, so self-assured, so fully herself, stirred something long dormant in me. I wanted to know her secret. I debated in my head whether it would be inappropriate to ask. Would I be crossing a line? Would she think I was projecting my insecurities onto her? I hesitated, caught in that all-too-familiar fear of taking up too much space. But something in me pushed past it. I approached her, heart pounding, and asked the question that had been burning in my chest: *How did you get here, this far up, without losing yourself?*

To my relief, her eyes softened with warmth. She smiled deeply, like she had been waiting for someone to ask. She told me the truth: for a long time, she *had* struggled with authenticity. She, too, had worn the mask, spoke the part, and played the game but eventually the cost became too high. She realized the very thing she feared – being seen for who she truly was – was the thing that gained her the most respect. Not from everyone, but from the right people. She said many of her white counterparts admired her for her authenticity. They trusted her more because she was honest, direct, and grounded. She told me, without hesitation, *"You don't need to be who they expect. You just need to be who you are. You've earned your seat at the table. Now take up space in it."*

That moment changed me. Her words pierced through the years of silence I'd internalized. I walked away from that conversation with a fire in my belly and a softness in my chest. For the first time, I realized I didn't have to choose between success and self. It was not only possible but necessary to bring all of me into the room. Piece by piece, I began reclaiming myself. I stopped overexplaining. I let my natural tone return. I wore my hair in ways that made me feel beautiful. I stopped apologizing for my brilliance, my boundaries, my Blackness. I stopped waiting for permission. Because I knew deep in my bones: the mask may get you in the room but you will never fully breathe while wearing it. I was ready to breathe. I was ready to live.

The woman I met that day was more than a leader. She was a mirror. She reminded me that being seen as I am is not a liability; it's liberation. From that moment forward, I committed to showing up whole. Not for them. For me. I loosened my grip on the mask and started to reclaim my voice, not all at once, but intentionally. Because I knew then, success without self is not success at all.

The Mask We Wear

Let's talk about the "mask." Have you ever walked into a new job eager, overqualified, and determined to prove you belonged? I have, and it didn't take long to realize being excellent wasn't enough. I quickly learned my credentials might open the door but my presence made people uncomfortable. I wasn't just managing projects and deadlines; I was managing perceptions. I had to manage not just my workload but their discomfort with my confidence. I had to balance my brilliance with humility, my voice with diplomacy, my presence with invisibility. I had to smile when I was distressed and laugh at things that weren't funny. I had to dim my light to keep others from feeling small.

What no one tells you is that wearing the mask starts off as a strategy, but over time it becomes suffocation. At first, it's subtle. You bite your tongue in meetings. You soften your tone, so you won't be labeled "difficult." You rehearse conversations in your head just to avoid confirming their biases. And then, one day, you look in the mirror and realize you've edited yourself so much, you don't recognize your own reflection. The mask molds to your face. It fits snug like a second skin, but it's heavy. It itches. It stifles. You begin to wonder if anyone at work knows who you really are, or if you even remember.

It's lonely behind the mask. You find yourself hyper-aware of everything: your tone, your posture, your word choice. You shrink in meetings when you know the answer, afraid of being "too assertive." You overwork, hoping being irreplaceable will make them overlook your Blackness. You listen to people praise your "professionalism," all while knowing they've never really seen *you*. You smile when your insides are screaming. You celebrate the wins with a tempered pride, because joy, real joy, requires freedom, and freedom doesn't live behind a mask.

And that, right there, is the lie we're sold: that we can be successful and fully ourselves in systems that were never designed to see us for who we are, that if we work hard enough, dress well enough, speak "professionally" enough, we'll be accepted. But the truth is, excellence isn't armor in these spaces. Often, it's the very thing making us a target. The truth is, many of us are working twice as hard in half the time, with a fraction of the recognition, while carrying the emotional labor of representing an entire race. Every word, every mistake, every moment of excellence is amplified, not just for ourselves, but for everyone who looks like us. It's exhausting, it's lonely, and it's unsustainable.

We become chameleons, shifting to survive, adjusting our tone of voice in meetings, and carefully curating our reactions. Wondering if we're being "too much" or "not enough." We start to internalize the idea we must choose between authenticity and advancement. But survival is not the same as living. I reached a point where I realized no amount of professional accolades was worth the cost of disconnecting from myself. No title, no paycheck, no seat at the table should require me to silence my truth.

These masks may keep us employed. They may keep the peace. But they also keep us small. And I've decided I don't want to live small anymore. I want to walk into every room as myself, fully and freely, not because it's easy, but because it's necessary. Because the world doesn't need another version of who they want us to be. It needs who we actually are. Unmasked. Unapologetic. Unafraid.

Burnout in Silence

Burnout doesn't always come with fanfare. Sometimes it comes with numbness. A slow, creeping detachment wrapping around your joy, your motivation, your purpose, until all that's left is going through the motions. It creeps in after another meeting where your ideas are ignored until someone else repeats them. Another microaggression passed off as a joke. Another performance review praising your "professionalism" but questioning your "attitude."

Burnout is when you start fantasizing about quitting but can't because your whole family is depending on you. Your children are watching. Your community is proud. You're the one who made it, and because of that, you feel like you have to keep making it, no matter the cost. It's when your soul is screaming, *This is not what I came here to do*, but your bills say otherwise. It's the gut-punch of realizing you've worked this hard for a title, salary, and seat at a table, only to feel like a stranger to yourself.

For Black women, burnout is not simply about being overworked. It's about being over-watched. Every move is under scrutiny. We're told to advocate for ourselves, but when we do, we're labeled aggressive. We're encouraged to "bring our full selves," but only if that self makes everyone else comfortable. When burnout shows up, when we falter, when our edges fray, we don't feel like we have the luxury to admit it because admitting burnout feels like admitting weakness. Like handing over confirmation to those silently waiting for us to slip, to prove what they already assumed: that we're not cut out for leadership, that we're too emotional, too ungrateful, too much.

So, we push through it. We work harder. Stay later. Smile wider. We sit in meetings with our voices trembling from exhaustion, praying no one notices the weight we're carrying. We overcompensate with excellence, terrified of being seen as incompetent if we say, *I'm tired. I'm overwhelmed. I need a break.* Because we know in the eyes of some, competence and perfection are the same thing, and anything less than perfection feels like a threat to our place at the table.

We suffer silently because we're afraid of what it would mean to walk away. Afraid of being labeled "ungrateful," "difficult," or "angry." Afraid of losing the opportunities we worked so hard for. Afraid admitting we're burnt out might be the very thing that pushes us out. But what about being free?

What about choosing yourself, not in the aftermath, not once you've collapsed, but *before* the breaking point? What about honoring the whisper before it becomes a scream? What about redefining competence as not just your ability to produce under pressure, but your capacity to protect your peace?

Burnout in silence is a slow erasure, a sacrifice serving everyone but you. We've done enough of that. We've carried this weight with grace. But grace should not require self-abandonment. It's time to remember you don't have to prove your worth through pain.

From Proving to Belonging

There's a moment in every Black woman's journey when the mask starts to choke her. When the weight of always being "on," always being poised, always being polished, becomes too much to bear. For me, that moment came quietly, yet forcefully, like a wave crashing into the shoreline of everything I thought I had built. I realized I was spending more time pretending to be okay than actually being okay. I mastered the art of high-functioning pain. I smiled and performed strength on demand. I kept going because stopping felt like failure, like giving up. People praised me for how well I "handled" everything, not realizing each compliment was like a stone added to the invisible load I was carrying. They saw composure; I felt collapse. I had become a professional version of myself, perfectly curated, meticulously contained, someone who looked impressive on paper but felt like a stranger in the mirror. My accomplishments were real, but so was the disconnection from my truth.

I spent so much time striving, perfecting, proving, just to be seen, just to be accepted, that I forgot I already had a right to be there. I'd already done the work. I'd already earned my seat. The degrees were mine. The sacrifices were real. The resilience wasn't a performance; it was lived. Every late night, every silent tear, every time I showed up while feeling broken, all of it built the foundation I stood on. It wasn't luck. It wasn't being "the exception." It was me. I had been so busy surviving I forgot I had already arrived. I didn't need to contort myself to fit into spaces I had outgrown spiritually and emotionally. I just needed to remember who I was before the world told me to be more palatable.

So, I had to stop performing and start reclaiming. Reclaiming my voice, the one stifled by fear, corporate culture, the haunting worry I might be "too much" or "not enough." Reclaiming my pace, because I no longer needed to run a race just to prove I belonged in rooms I already earned my way into. Reclaiming my boundaries, because my value isn't measured by how much I can endure in silence. Reclaiming my joy, because joy is my birthright, not a reward for how much I've suffered. I realized success means nothing if it costs you your sanity, your softness, your soul. And the deeper truth? I was never meant to fit into a system requiring me to erase myself. I wasn't an outsider hoping for permission; I was the blueprint. I was always deserving. I was always enough.

I was meant to build new systems rooted in truth, equity, rest, deliverance, and the full, unapologetic expression of who I am. I no longer wait for gatekeepers to tell me I'm allowed in. I know now: every room I've entered, every space I've shown up in, every position I've fought for, I didn't stumble there. I built myself up to walk through those doors, and I belong there just as much as anyone else, period. It's time to silence the voice of impostor syndrome that tries to shrink us. That voice is not our own; it's the echo of generations of exclusion and erasure. We are rewriting that narrative. We are reclaiming what's always been ours.

It's time to embrace the truth of our brilliance, our labor, our resilience, and our *divinity*. A Black woman doesn't have to outperform to be worthy. She doesn't have to harden herself to be respected. She doesn't have to minimize her magic to make others comfortable. She is already powerful. She is already brilliant. She is already whole. That is not arrogance; it is truth. And living in that truth without apology? That is real power. That is real freedom.

Redefining Success

I realized success is no longer about the title. It's about the truth. It's no longer about who validates me; it's about how I validate myself. It's no longer about the table; it's about whether I feel nourished when I sit there. Now, I work in alignment with my soul, not in reaction to systems that never saw me to begin with.

I've learned letting go of corporate respectability doesn't mean letting go of ambition. Respectability has always been there, wrapped in envy. It means redefining ambition on your own terms. It means knowing that your worth isn't up for negotiation. It means taking off the chameleon skin and walking in your full, radiant, Black woman power, thanks to that Black girl magic.

I saw this truth clearly when I was in line to become a Flight Commander. As a Physician Assistant in the military, those roles aren't handed out to us. We're trained to be the workhorses of military medicine, exceptional clinicians, but must fight for real leadership. After twenty years of service, and six of those grinding under impossible workloads, I was finally an Element Leader, preparing to step into Flight Command. It was a breakthrough, a moment I had prepared myself for.

Then, just a month before the transition, a younger nurse with no leadership experience arrived. She was soft-spoken, eager to please, and unfamiliar with our clinic's unique mission. Still, she was chosen. I knew instantly her presence had been strategically placed, not for impact or mission readiness but for compliance. She didn't understand the weight of what we were carrying, the burnout, the relentless sacrifice, the emotional labor required to keep our team and mission afloat. While she, too, was a Black woman, it was clear she didn't align herself with Us. She served power, not people. She smiled in rooms where injustice thrived, looked at me with that mix of silent disdain and studied politeness, an echo of the very systems that prize obedience over authenticity.

She reported to the high command behind my back, challenging my place in leadership. It's funny how I was still the Element Leader, still guiding operations, and remained the most experienced provider in the clinic, with intimate knowledge of its past, present, and future mission goals. The previous Flight Commander had been preparing me to take command. Instead of working with me to learn, she rejected the Flight Commander and Element Leader relationship, impairing our ability to focus on the mission and our personnel. I watched morale crumble under her command. The spark drained from my team's eyes, and the weight of guilt, coupled with her sabotage of my character, broke me. I had poured myself into that clinic, worked side by side with our previous Commander to build a space that honored both people and mission. Now it was unraveling.

Eventually, I threw in the towel and stepped away. I was moved to another clinic and I took it as a failure. It felt like I had abandoned my people. But six months later, something miraculous happened: I could breathe again. The bags under my eyes disappeared. I could take lunch breaks. I finished my doctorate. I showed up for my family in ways I hadn't in years. My stress plummeted, and in that stillness, I heard my own voice again. I was approached by the Flight Commander at that clinic and asked to be an Element Leader. The weapon formed against me became a doorway onto a parallel path, one of peace and reduced stress, with my same leadership position.

I realized success wasn't lost; it had just changed form. I found it in my peace. I found it in freedom. People still came to me, venting about what they had to endure under the new leadership, wishing I had stayed. But I'd already found what I was looking for. Success, for me, wasn't the position. It was the preservation of my purpose. The restoration of my joy. The reclamation of my time. That hidden force, the one that rerouted me when I thought I had failed, wasn't my enemy. It was grace. And grace will always lead you back to yourself.

Reflection

Reflect on who you've had to become to survive in professional spaces. What parts of your identity have you muted, reshaped, or hidden to fit in or be deemed "professional"? Think about the internal negotiations you've made just to be palatable. Now, consider what authenticity looks like in those same spaces. What would it mean to stop performing and start honoring your whole self, even at work?

Chapter 6
THE BURDEN OF BEING STRONG

"They called me strong before they ever asked if I was okay."

Resilience has been our badge of honor. It's what they admire most about us: our ability to endure, to rise, to hold it down no matter what. But nobody asks what it costs. We live in a world that applauds our adaptability while ignoring our pain. A culture that praises our independence but doesn't hold space for our exhaustion. A society that depends on our strength but is indifferent to our suffering. This chapter is not an indictment of strength; our strength is sacred. It is an invitation to express how tired we are. Not just physically – we are soul tired. This resilience has become a mask we can't take off, even when we're drowning.

It's the kind of tired sleep can't fix. The kind that sits in your bones and makes everything feel heavier. We smile through it. We show up anyway. We give from an empty cup because we've been taught rest is weakness and asking for help is a sign of failure. Even when we're praised for being "strong Black women," the weight of that label is often just a beautiful way to ignore our pain. We carry generations of unspoken grief, of holding families together, of enduring workplaces that drain us, of being everything to everyone, except ourselves. Sometimes, I've found myself breaking down privately in parking lots and bathrooms, because there was no room to fall apart publicly. Being strong has become a role we didn't ask for but learn to play flawlessly.

I remember coming home after work, exhausted from the day. Patient care isn't a physically demanding job. It's emotionally and mentally demanding. Sunday nights became a slow ache, a sadness that crept in as the sun set. I would dread Monday before it even arrived. The routine was relentless. I'd wake up at five in the morning, sometimes to clean, sometimes to start a load of laundry, sometimes to squeeze in a quick workout before I began the day. Then came the rush, getting the kids up, dressed, and out the door before heading to work myself. I'd often sit in the parking lot, eyes closed, trying to meditate and clear my mind just enough to take in what I knew was waiting for me: the emotions, the trauma, the expectations of my patients.

From 7:30 a.m. onward, every twenty minutes, someone new entered my exam room, bringing not just their physical complaints but also years of pain, anxiety, fear, and frustration. The game of "guess that diagnosis" would begin, often with patients who had already consulted "Dr. Google" and wanted confirmation rather than care. I spent hours not just treating symptoms, but managing egos, navigating entitlement, and sometimes defending my own expertise, especially when my diagnosis was questioned solely because I was a Black woman. There were days when a white male patient would flat-out dismiss my assessment, only to return later to receive the same diagnosis from someone who looked more like them. The emotional labor of being strong, competent, and composed in the face of casual bias was crushing.

Still, I stayed. Because that's what strong Black women do. We keep showing up. I've learned the expectation of endless resilience is killing us softly. What's worse is that the moment we try to step back, to breathe, to say "I can't today," we're met with confusion, disappointment, or guilt, as if strength has made us less human, as if we owe our unbreakable spirit to the world at all costs. But we don't. We are allowed to rest, to cry, to say, "This is too much." None of that makes us less worthy or less powerful. In fact, it brings us back to our truth.

True strength isn't found in how much we can carry alone, it's found in our ability to release, receive, and remember we are worthy of care, too. This chapter is the call to put the armor down, not forever, but long enough to breathe. Long enough to feel. Long enough to remember strength should never cost us our wholeness.

The Myth That Keeps Us Bound

The "Strong Black Woman" archetype was born out of necessity. It wasn't a title we asked for; it was one we inherited. When no one came to save us, we saved ourselves. When the world dehumanized us, stripped our names, languages, children, and agency, we found power in our survival. We rose from fields soaked with sweat and blood, through the aching silence of loss, through centuries of being unseen and unheard. We took the pieces of our brokenness and built homes, raised nations, and birthed revolutions. That strength was never a costume; it was our protective breastplate, forged in the fire of resilience, sharpened by generations of pain. Somewhere along the line, that resilience stopped being a tool for survival and became a mandate. What began as a means of endurance evolved into a performance. Our vulnerability, our softness, and our need for support were no longer welcome. We weren't allowed to just be; we had to be everything. We had to be strong.

We were no longer permitted to ask for help, no longer permitted to rest, and no longer allowed to fall apart. We became superhuman to everyone but ourselves. We were the backbones of communities and secret keepers of generations, but we were not allowed to cry. We were not allowed to say, "I'm tired," or "I can't." Because being strong became the role we were expected to play every single day, without fail, without exception, without room to breathe, when we dared to show even a flicker of our true selves, our exhaustion, our grief, our need, we were met with confusion or contempt. "But you're so strong," they said, as if strength could silence our pain, as if a compliment could erase our humanity.

They praised our strength, but only when it served them. They weaponized it. "You're so strong" became the reason we were overlooked for help. "You're so strong" became the excuse to place more on our shoulders. "You're so strong" became the permission to ignore our boundaries, to push past our limits, to demand our silence. It meant our pain could be dismissed, our burnout misunderstood, our depression unseen. It meant our labor could be extracted without recognition; our loyalty expected without reciprocation.

What's more heartbreaking is that we began to believe it. We swallowed the myth whole, letting it live in our bones. We felt guilty for needing rest, ashamed for needing help, unworthy if we weren't carrying someone else's burden. We mistook constant self-sacrifice for love, silence for grace, and endurance for identity.

This isn't just a modern story; it is an ancestral one. It reaches back to the ships, to the auction blocks, to the plantations where our foremothers were stripped of everything and still found a way to survive. Their hearts had to harden to endure the unthinkable: rape, violence, children ripped from their arms, labor forced through tears. They learned how to wear masks, how to laugh through pain, how to find God in suffering. They were never given the luxury of breaking down. They had to keep going because the cost of stopping was death. So, the strength they modeled was never softness denied; it was softness stolen. We've inherited that same unrelenting spirit, generation after generation, until it wrapped itself around our identities like a shroud.

How do we find ourselves beneath all that weight? How do we even begin to imagine softness when the world only rewards our hardness? How do we reclaim our need for gentleness when we've been conditioned to call it weakness? The truth is this myth never protected us; it caged us. It convinced us that suffering was our birthright. That silence was noble. That being everything to everyone else was the only way we mattered. But we are not here to bleed in silence. We are not here to bend until we break. We are not here to be the world's backbone while our own hearts fracture.

We are allowed to rest. We are allowed to weep. We are allowed to say no. We are allowed to ask for more. None of that makes us less Black, less powerful, or less divine. In fact, that's where our true strength begins, in the truth of our full humanity. Not in being invincible, but in being whole. Because we are not myths. We are not archetypes. We are women. We are people. We deserve to be held with the same tenderness we have always given. This is our declaration: no more carrying the world on broken backs, no more smiling through sorrow to make others comfortable, and no more performing a strength that costs us our souls.

Let this be our return to ourselves, to softness, to the truth, and to rest. Let this be our rebellion: choosing wholeness in a world that only sees our utility. Because being fully human in a society that wants you to be a machine is the most powerful thing we can ever do.

The Invisible Labor of Holding It All Together

Behind every "strong Black woman" is a list of invisible jobs she never applied for, roles inherited through survival and passed down like heirlooms from grandmothers who carried the world on their backs without ever being asked if they were tired. We're the emotional anchors of our families, expected to be unshakable when storms hit, even if we're struggling inside. We become the unofficial therapists to our friends, the ones who listen and affirm, who hold space and offer healing, even when there's no one to do the same for us. We are the community organizers, advocates for change, steadfast caretakers, the first to show up, the last to rest. At work, we are the go-to problem solvers, the quiet experts who clean up messes and fix chaos, and still manage to perform at an excellent level, only to have our ideas stolen or ignored. We're the financial backbones, the ones who send money back home, pay the bills, cover the gaps, and somehow keep a smile on our faces. We are the keepers of peace, navigating family drama, workplace tension, social unrest, and emotional disconnection, asked to be the bridge, the balm, the solution.

And all the while, we are pouring – pouring from our bodies, our spirits, and our gifts – into children, partners, elders, coworkers, churches, and communities, pouring and pouring, yet rarely, if ever, being poured into. Even our joy is policed. If we laugh too loud, we're ghetto. If we celebrate ourselves, we're arrogant. Our softness is questioned, seen as a weakness, a liability, a betrayal of the myth we're built to endure anything. Even our rest is judged, as if the world only respects us when we're grinding ourselves to dust. We are allowed to succeed, but not to soften. To lead, but not to lean. To help, but never to hurt. If we dare to show cracks in the armor, dare to say, "I need," "I'm worn-out," or "this is too much," we are met with disbelief, or worse, shame. As if strength has become our only currency, or being exhausted is a prerequisite for being loved.

Who holds the strong Black woman when she's tired of being strong? Who sees her beyond her usefulness? Who lets her cry without demanding she explain herself or apologize for the tears? Who says, "You don't have to hold it all today. You can rest now. You deserve to be cared for, too." The truth is, beneath the layers of excellence and endurance is a woman with wounds. A woman with a heart that's been broken a thousand times but still beats with hope. A woman who has shown up for everyone but herself. A woman who wonders, in the quiet moments, what it would feel like to be held the way she holds the world.

This labor we do, this invisible, unpaid, unspoken labor, is not just physical. It is soul labor. It is the labor of pretending to be okay. The labor of not scaring white coworkers with our grief or our rage. The labor of keeping the family together after funerals, divorces, evictions, and disappointments. The labor of never letting our children see us crumble. The labor of making miracles out of not enough. It is holy, yes, but it is also heavy. While we may continue to show up, to serve, to lead, we must no longer pretend this weight doesn't come at a cost. We must no longer believe we are only valuable when we are producing, fixing, saving, or sacrificing. We are worthy even in our stillness. We are sacred even when we stop. We deserve lives that allow us to breathe, to be cared for, to be soft, and to be whole.

Letting Go of the Performance

I was praised for being dependable, but I was hurting. I was admired for being unshakable, but I was numb. I was thanked for being "the rock," but I was crumbling inside. No one ever noticed the quiet ways I was unraveling. I never let them. I learned how to hide it too well. I showed up for everyone, everywhere, all the time, with a full face and an empty soul. My strength wasn't wholeness; it was survival. It was a carefully constructed mask I wore so the world wouldn't see how deeply I was breaking because being strong wasn't just something I did. It was something I believed I had to be to deserve love, respect, and even basic care.

Letting go of that role was one of the hardest things I've ever done, because who are you if you're not the strong one? Who are you if your identity has been wrapped in resilience, and suddenly you're too tired to keep holding it all? Who are you if you say, "I can't," instead of "I got it"? Who are you if you fall apart in front of people who've only ever known your power, but never your pain? I was terrified to find out. I feared that if I stopped performing, I'd be abandoned. That the love I had earned by being useful would disappear if I wasn't holding everyone else together. I feared vulnerability would be met with judgment, not compassion.

I was wrong. When I finally let go, when I cracked open and let the truth spill out, I met a deeper version of myself. One who was tender. One who was tired. One who was worthy of love, even when she wasn't holding up the sky. You are still you, even when you say, "I need help." You are still valuable when you admit, "I can't keep doing this." You are still deserving when you choose yourself over expectations that never made room for your rest, your grief, your healing. You are human. You are worthy.

Strength is not the absence of vulnerability. It's not swallowing your pain to keep the peace. It's not saying "yes" when your soul is crying out for "no." Real strength is being honest about what you need, even if your voice trembles. It's sitting with your tears and letting them fall without shame. It's reaching out instead of retreating. It's letting go of the cape you never should've had to wear and whispering, "Today, I choose me." Not because you're selfish. But because you're sacred. And that sacredness deserves tending, softness, and relaxation. You don't have to keep breaking yourself down to be seen. You do not have to keep performing strength to be loved. You are enough, exactly as you are. And maybe the bravest thing you'll ever do is not holding it all together but finally allowing yourself to fall apart and be held.

Softness is Revolutionary

In a world that demands our toughness, softness becomes a radical act. We were never meant to be stone, but survival taught us to harden, to brace ourselves for impact, to lead with our armor instead of our hearts. We learned vulnerability was dangerous, rest was laziness, and being "the strong one" was the only way we'd be protected, accepted, or respected. So, we put on the cape, built the walls, silenced our cries, and carried it all. But beneath the strength was always a yearning, a whisper in the soul that said, *"There has to be more than this."*

Choosing rest is a form of rebellion. Choosing peace is a form of healing. Choosing ourselves, softly, intentionally, without apology, is a form of freedom. It means letting go of the false belief love must be earned through suffering. It means releasing the performance and coming home to our truth: that softness is not weakness, but sacred strength. That to be soft is to be open. And to be open is to finally allow ourselves to be loved the way we deserve.

When we embrace our softness, we stop auditioning for love and start receiving it. We begin to understand we're worthy of tenderness, of affection, of a love that doesn't require us to shrink, hustle, or prove. We become emotionally available, not just to others, but to ourselves. Because softness makes space for connection, it lets us be seen beyond our accomplishments. It allows us to be held when we're tired. It teaches us how to communicate what we need, how to ask for it without shame, and how to receive love without suspicion or guilt. Softness allows us to let our guards down, to trust, and to stop confusing control with safety.

Romantic love, real love, cannot thrive behind walls built by pain. It needs breath, room, and intimacy. When we are locked in survival mode, we often mistake independence for protection, but it ultimately becomes isolation. We can do it all, yes, but we don't have to. Softness says, *"I want to share this life with someone."* It says, *"I deserve partnership, not performance."* It opens the door to loving and being loved with honesty, depth, and reciprocity. And it teaches others how to love us in return, not as pillars of strength, but as whole, feeling, deserving women.

You don't have to be "on" all the time. You don't have to prove your worth through pain. You don't have to carry everyone and everything. You are allowed to be messy, tender, healing, and whole. You are allowed to rest. To cry. You are allowed to let someone else carry you sometimes. It is safe to put the armor down, to open your heart. In the breaking, we make space for something new – *freedom*. That freedom brings with it a love that sees you fully, holds you gently, and honors you deeply, not because of how strong you are, but because you are finally allowing yourself to be soft enough to receive it.

Softness is not the end of your strength; it's the beginning of your restoration. It's about making room for joy, for peace, for deep, nourishing love. The kind of love that doesn't want your mask or your cape, just your heart.

Reflection

Ask yourself what it has cost to be "the strong one." Who benefits from your strength, and what has it kept you from receiving? Think about the ways you've been rewarded for self-denial, for silence, for pushing through. What does strength look like now that you're healing? What if it looked more like softness, boundaries, or asking for help?

Part II
THE WORK OF BECOMING

"Healing is not linear. Becoming is messy, brave, and sacred work."

This section marks the heart of the journey, the work it takes to shed old wounds, reclaim sacred parts of ourselves, and build new foundations. This is where the deep unraveling begins. It's where we stop surviving by default and start becoming by intention. Because to truly let go, we must first become the version of ourselves strong enough to release what we've been carrying. We can't drop the weight if we're still tangled in it. We must become someone who no longer needs the armor, the over-functioning, the silence, or the struggle to feel worthy.

Becoming is not just a process; it's a homecoming. It's the sacred act of choosing yourself again and again, even when the path back to you feels unfamiliar. This work isn't always visible. It's the quiet discipline of showing up for your healing when no one's watching. It's crying in your car, setting boundaries you once feared, or waking up and telling yourself the truth. Some days it feels like freedom, other days like grief. However, all of it is part of the process of becoming.

We must honor the brave, messy, beautiful process of evolving beyond pain and limitation, not by pretending those things never shaped us, but by refusing to let them define us. Here, we begin to build a life that holds space for our happiness, our softness, our power, and our truth. We reconnect with spirit in ways that nourish, rather than deplete. We confront the stories we've been told, and the ones we've told ourselves about money, love, and self-worth. And then we write new ones. We trade survival for sustainability. Hustle for harmony; scarcity for sovereignty.

We also return to something ancient: community, sisterhood, chosen family. The kind of connection that doesn't require translation or performance. In these spaces, we remember we're not alone in our becoming. Healing can be a collective act. A future waits for us, one we get to co-create.

Chapter 7
A LOVE LETTER TO MY SPIRIT

"I am more than the faith I was taught. I am the fire of my ancestors, the divine in my bones."

I was taught to pray with my eyes closed and my hands folded, to fear hell more than I trusted heaven, and that God was a man in the sky, watching my every move, waiting to correct me. What I wasn't taught was that Spirit lived in me. The divine didn't just visit on Sunday mornings. But instead, the spirit of God could pulse through my breath, my body, my bloodline, and sound like a drumbeat, feel like a dance, or come through a dream.

This chapter is a reclamation and return, a reminder your spirit doesn't have to fit inside the boxes it was given. I didn't grow up hearing I was sacred. I heard I was strong. I heard I was smart. I heard I was "blessed and highly favored," even when I was barely holding myself together. But no one told me I could find God in myself, that Spirit doesn't require perfection to dwell in me. That I don't have to be endlessly obedient, endlessly apologetic, endlessly performing goodness just to be worthy of love.

There's a difference between religion and relationship. I followed the rules. I stayed in line. I memorized scriptures that told me to obey, to suffer quietly, to be patient through the pain. Inside, my spirit was restless. My soul spoke a language no one around me could translate. I felt guilty for questioning. I felt wrong for longing for more. The more I lived, the more I realized I had been worshiping with a gag order over my truth. What I had been taught to call reverence was sometimes fear in disguise and I'd internalized a version of God that only approved of me when I was exhausted, when I was self-sacrificing, when I was disappearing for others.

My spirit began to stretch the moment I gave myself permission to feel the spirit and stop parroting beliefs. I began to notice how divinity showed up in the everyday: the way the wind whispered comfort when I was grieving, how music wrapped around me like a prayer when words failed, and how dreams carried messages my waking mind wasn't ready to receive.

I began to trust that if I come from God, nothing about me was accidental. Not my voice. Not my rage. Not my tenderness. Not my desire to be free. I started listening to my intuition not as something suspicious, but sacred. I started honoring my body not as something sinful, but as a sanctuary. I let go of trying to be holy according to someone else's blueprint and started becoming whole on my own terms.

This love letter to my spirit is also an apology to the parts of me I silenced, doubted, and dismissed. To the little girl who wondered if her questions meant she was broken. To the woman who mistook fear for faith and shame for humility. I'm sorry – and I'm grateful. Despite everything, you never gave up on me.

This chapter is not about turning away from God. It's about turning inward to the divine in me, around me, and before me. The God of our grandmother's garden, the one who heard the prayers we couldn't put into words, the one who met me in the mirror when I finally looked at myself with love instead of judgment. The one who reminds me daily: I am already enough. You do not have to earn sacredness. You are sacred because you exist. You are not too complicated, too loud, too questioning, too emotional, or too much.

You are the evidence of everything your ancestors prayed for, danced for, and cried for. You are the altar and the offering.

May this be your invitation to reconnect with the Spirit that has always been with you, not to fit into faith, but to embody it. Not to ask for permission, but to walk in your divine birthright. May your path be your own and may your spirit finally feel at home.

Reclaiming Spiritual Identity

For many Black women, spirituality has been shaped by complex intersections, colonial religion, generational beliefs, personal trauma, and ancestral traditions often silenced or demonized. These intersections are not just theological. They are lived. They are etched into our memories, our family histories, and the rituals we were taught to either fear or forget. Our spiritual foundation has often been laid on top of inherited wounds, where salvation was offered but freedom was conditional.

Some of us grew up in churches that taught obedience more than self-love, where we were taught to serve but not to listen to ourselves. Where submission was sacred, and questioning was sinful. We memorized scriptures about love while rarely feeling truly seen or safe. We were handed faith that sometimes felt like a cage, adorned in hope but closed off from our complexity.

Some of us were told our intuition was "worldly." That the deep, quiet knowing within us was suspect, untrustworthy, even demonic. That the gifts we carried, our dreams, our sensitivity, our connection to the unseen, were dangerous if not sanctioned by someone else's interpretation of truth. We learned to silence ourselves, to defer, to ignore the whisper within that often knew better than the voices around us.

Some of us were punished for asking too many questions or wanting something different. We were told we were "too curious," "too fast," or "too bold." But really, we were seeking something more honest. Something with room for both pain and power. Something that didn't ask us to disappear to be holy.

Our spirit never stopped speaking, even when we stopped listening, when we were told to pray louder instead of feeling deeper, when we were too afraid to admit we were confused, or disillusioned, or distant from the God we'd been told to worship. Spirit kept showing up in our tears, our dreams, and the way our bodies would tense when something wasn't right. In the silence, it spoke clearly.

Reclaiming your spiritual identity means making space for your own truth, even if it doesn't match what you were taught. It means being brave enough to sit with your own questions, to unlearn what no longer fits, and to honor what you now know to be true. It's a deeply personal journey that can feel lonely at times, especially when you're breaking generational contracts around faith. It is also where your soul begins to breathe again. It means listening to the quiet voice within that says: *I don't need to perform to be holy. I don't need to shrink, strive, or sacrifice my wholeness for belonging. Holiness is not how well I hide my truth, but how fully I live in it.* Reclaiming your spirituality is not about discarding everything from your past; it's about discerning. Keeping what nurtures your soul and releasing what starves it. It's about embracing your body, your story, your knowing as sacred ground.

This is not about rejecting religion, but about liberating yourself spiritually. Permitting yourself to build a spiritual practice that feels like home, not an obligation. One that honors the sacredness of your ancestors and the truth of your lived experience.

It's about remembering no one can define your relationship with the divine but you. Your connection to God doesn't require translation or validation. It's already yours. It always has been.

Ask yourself: *What parts of my faith feel true, and what parts feel forced? What does it look like to honor God/Spirit/Source in my own language, on my own terms?* You are not lost; you are returning to the wisdom that was buried but never broken, returning to the voice that's been waiting for you to hear it, and returning to a faith that feels like you.

Ancestral Connection

Long before colonization, our ancestors knew Spirit intimately. They didn't need permission or doctrine to access the divine; they were in constant conversation with the world around them. They spoke to the earth with bare feet planted in soil rich with memory. They listened to the wind like it carried messages just for them. They honored the moon as if it were an elder, steady and sacred, cycling through darkness and light as we all do. They lit candles not just for ambiance but for guidance. They poured libations with steady hands, whispering names of those who came before. They sang to the stars with voices hoarse from labor but full of soul, knowing the night sky held the dreams of generations. They healed with their hands, rooted in intuition, plants, prayers, and with hearts that carried the wisdom of lineages long before us.

This wisdom lives in you. Even if you've never been taught how to access it, even if time and trauma have created distance between you and the rituals of your people, it waits patiently within you. You may feel it rise unexpectedly, in the goosebumps that crawl up your arms when a particular song plays, or in the heavy silence that falls over a room when you speak a truth your great-grandmother never could. You may hear it in your dreams, in languages you don't speak but somehow understand. You may see it reflected in your mother's eyes or feel it in your aunties' unspoken strength. You may not know the rituals exactly, but your soul remembers. Even when the body forgets, the blood remembers.

That remembering is sacred. It's not performative. It's not about getting it perfect. It's about allowing your body to recognize itself in the legacy it carries. Reconnecting with your ancestors means coming face-to-face with what has been lost, what was hidden, and what was once punished. It also means reclaiming what still belongs to you: dignity, protection, and an inheritance of spiritual brilliance that predates slavery, shame, or silence.

Ancestral connection is about intentionally honoring those who came before you, not just in moments of mourning, but in moments of joy and the quiet of ordinary days. It might look like setting up an altar in the corner of your home, filled with photos, cloth, flowers, or objects that feel like memories. It might mean lighting a single candle and whispering their names into the stillness, calling them near. It might mean cooking their food from memory, even if you must guess the ingredients, and telling their stories while you stir. It might be as simple as placing your hand on your heart and asking, "What do you want me to remember?" And it might also be unspoken, a presence you feel while walking alone, a knowing that sits with you in moments of deep clarity or unshakable peace. Your ancestors do not require perfection to show up. They ask only for presence. For reverence. For you to live in a way honoring the sacrifices they made for you, even to be here. Every time you heal, every time you choose softness over survival, every time you allow yourself to be fully human, you do what some of them never had the chance to.

You are not alone on your path. You are walking with an entire lineage behind you. You are never just one person standing in a moment. You are the result of dreams, prayers, battles, and blessings passed through wombs, whispered through generations, and woven into your very being. When you truly begin to tap into that connection, you feel something shift. You don't just feel supported; you feel sovereign, grounded, and whole. Not because you've become someone new but because you've finally remembered who you've always been.

Divine Feminine Energy

In many of the religious traditions we were raised in, God was male. Authority was male. Power was male. Those images were held up as the blueprint for righteousness. Anything that didn't reflect them – so much of who we were – was treated as lesser, even sinful. But you, Black woman, are not an accident.

Your intuition, your softness, your tears, your womb, your wisdom – they are not flaws. They are holy. You were born with a knowing the world tried to train out of you. The instinct to feel deeply, to listen inwardly, to tend to what cannot be seen but always sensed, was never weakness. It was divine instruction.

The divine feminine is not weak. She is the creator, the nurturer, the destroyer, and the healer. She is not confined to gentleness. She is layered and complex. She holds space for grief and joy at the same time. She is fierce when she needs to protect and tender when it's time to rest. She exists in stillness, movement, mystery, and clarity.

She is present in the way we care for our children and elders, in the way we observe our inner world without rushing through it, and in how we attune ourselves to what is unspoken. She shows up when we let ourselves feel without justification, when we center pleasure without guilt, when we create without asking for permission. She reminds us power and softness do not live on opposite ends of a spectrum; they live within each other.

Embracing your divine feminine means trusting your emotions as signals, not problems. It means honoring rest, not just productivity. It means embracing your sensuality without shame. It means allowing yourself to be witnessed in your fullness, rather than reducing yourself to make others more comfortable.

This sacred feminine energy is your inheritance. It was passed down in prayers whispered under breath, in the way your mother's hands moved through your hair, in the ancestral pull that rises in your chest when you know something is true, without needing anyone else to validate it. It is the quiet power that's always lived in your body, waiting for your permission to unfold.

To harness this energy, start by slowing down, not as an indulgence, but as a radical act of remembrance. Carve out space for rituals that nourish your spirit: take cleansing baths, adorn your body with intention, dance without needing rhythm, write yourself into clarity. Practice listening to your womb energy, its signals, its wisdom, its cycles. Say no when you mean no, and yes only when it honors you. Touch your body with reverence. Speak your needs without apology. Let your creative energy flow through writing, painting, cooking, singing, however your spirit wants to express. Let your joy be unmeasured and your boundaries non-negotiable.

The divine feminine is not a costume to wear; it is a return to your most authentic self. It is the remembrance you are sacred because you exist. You are not here to shrink. You are here to expand. You are here to embody the fullness of your humanity and divinity, without needing to prove or perform. You are here to trust that what flows through you is not only worthy but holy.

Let this be the moment you choose to stop withholding your tenderness, your intuition, your sacred no, your powerful yes. Let this be the moment you remember: You were never too much. You were never not enough. You were divine all along.

Finding Safety in Self

There is a particular exhaustion that comes from constantly assessing whether you are too much or not enough. It wears on the spirit in subtle, relentless ways, creating a quiet pressure to dilute, contort, or prove yourself. Many of us have spent years learning how to shape-shift just enough to feel tolerated, if not fully seen. Safety, for so long, has felt like a reward you earn, not a birthright you return to. We learned to chase it through perfectionism, silence, staying small or hypervigilant. We learned to keep the peace at the expense of our own. But spiritual liberation asks a different question: *What would it mean to feel safe, right now, exactly as you are?*

Finding safety in self means stepping outside the loop of seeking permission. It is no longer organizing your existence around the fear of being misunderstood, misjudged, or rejected. It means choosing, day by day, not to fragment yourself to fit into someone else's comfort zone. It's choosing not to leave your body, your voice, or your truth just to be more palatable. It's a tender, often quiet revolution, rooted in the sacred act of staying with yourself. Even when others don't. Especially when others don't. It is not selfish. It is sacred.

There's power in being able to say, *I know what I feel, and I trust that it matters.* That clarity doesn't come from the outside. It emerges when you start turning inward with curiosity instead of criticism. When you stop measuring your value by how well you can be everything for everyone and instead begin tending to yourself like someone worth protecting.

To build that kind of safety, you start by listening differently, not to the expectations projected onto you or the inner critic mimicking old voices of shame, but to the subtler truths housed within your own body. You notice the tension that creeps into your jaw when you're biting back your truth. The way your stomach knots when you say yes but mean no. The dull ache in your chest when you've gone too long without rest, without touch, without joy. You notice, and then you honor.

You respond to yourself with presence, not punishment. With patience, not pressure. You begin to create small rituals of returning things that feel like home to your nervous system. A few minutes of stillness in the morning before the world's demands flood in. Placing your hand over your heart when anxiety surfaces, as if to say, "I'm not abandoning you." Taking a breath before responding to someone, asking yourself first, *What do I need right now?*

Some days, this self-trust might look like canceling plans without guilt. Other days, it might mean saying what's true for you, even when your voice trembles. It may be holding space for sadness without needing to fix it or celebrating joy without needing a reason. It may mean turning your phone off, turning your music on, and remembering solitude is not loneliness, it is communion. Eventually, something shifts. The need to overexplain softens. The urge to prove quiets. And what's left is a steadiness that no one else has to validate. That's the kind of safety we were never taught but always needed. It allows you to hold discomfort without falling apart, builds trust with yourself. It's not about being unaffected by the world; it's about learning how to come back to yourself no matter what the world tries to strip away.

Let that be your quiet revolution: to live rooted in your own truth, and to let that truth be enough. Let it be the soil where your wholeness takes root, not because someone else finally saw you, but because *you* did.

Take a moment to check in with your spirit – not your

productivity, image, or performance, but with your

innermost self. When was the last time you asked yourself

what you truly needed, not just to function, but to feel alive?

Think about how you can begin tending to your spirit with

the same urgency you've given to everything and everyone

else.

Chapter 8

THE CURRENCY OF FREEDOM

"Money is energy. I am reclaiming mine, not to survive, but to thrive."

For so many Black women, money has never felt neutral. It's been emotionally tied to survival and sacrifice. Sometimes it was the reason we kept our heads down when we wanted to speak up. Sometimes it was the unspoken tension in the room, the reason our mothers clenched their jaws at the grocery store or worked through chronic pain without ever calling out. It's been a story passed down through glances, through grit, through the constant push to "make do" and never complain. We've seen money withheld from us as a punishment.

We've seen it used to silence our needs or manipulate our futures. We've witnessed it elevate those who don't work half as hard and bypass those who carry entire families on their backs.

We've also witnessed how conversations about wealth often exclude us entirely or include us only when the story is one of struggle. We've watched institutions capitalize on our labor, our loyalty, our culture, while offering us scraps and expecting gratitude. We've been conditioned to believe wanting more, more ease, more comfort, more ownership, was greedy or unrealistic. That financial security was reserved for someone else, somewhere else, with a life more stable, more deserving and palatable.

This chapter is about changing that story. It's about confronting the internal and external lies we've been fed about money: what we're allowed to want, what we're supposed to settle for, and who we believe ourselves to be when the paycheck runs out. It's about reclaiming money as a tool of sovereignty, not a weapon of shame. A source of choice, not chains. Because you deserve more than enough, not as a reward for your suffering, but as a legacy. You deserve to rest without guilt. You deserve to experience beauty, joy, and care, not just on holidays or birthdays, but every day.

You deserve to make decisions from a place of peace, not panic. To leave jobs that drain you, to say no to partnerships that diminish you, to give generously without emptying yourself in the process. You deserve a relationship with money that feels ethical, soul-honoring, and expansive, reflecting your values and your vision, not someone else's definition of success.

This is not about greed. This is about restoration. About disentangling your worth from your wage and dismantling the belief you must prove, perform, or persevere beyond reason just to earn a sense of security. It's about naming the trauma money has carried through your lineage and choosing to break that cycle with compassion and clarity. It's about learning to feel safe with money. To hold it, manage it, circulate it, without fear that it will vanish, or that you are unworthy of keeping it.

The truth is, many of us have been taught how to stretch a dollar, but not how to receive with ease. We've been taught how to survive scarcity, but not how to hold abundance without self-sabotage or guilt. That's what this chapter calls us to unlearn.

Wealth is not just about accumulation, it's about liberation. It's about knowing you can rest, create, breathe, and build without being at the mercy of systems never designed for your thriving. When you begin to see money as a sacred partner, not your master or your enemy, you stop abandoning yourself to chase it. You stop shrinking your needs to accommodate its absence. You begin to trust that you are allowed to want more. That you are capable of stewarding more. That you are ready to receive more.

The currency of freedom is not just found in your bank account. It's in your ability to choose rest when you're tired. To walk away from what no longer honors you. To create a life that reflects your truth, not your trauma, and that kind of wealth, that deep, soul-aligned, liberating wealth, is your inheritance to reclaim.

Let this be the moment you stop apologizing for wanting ease. Let this be the season you stop confusing struggle with virtue. You are allowed to have money and still be soft, still be spiritual, still be rooted. You are allowed to have enough, and more than enough. Because your flourishing is not selfish; it's sacred.

Building Generational Wealth

Generational wealth is not just about passing down money. It's about passing down choice, opportunity, and freedom. That kind of freedom, the kind where your children don't have to recover from what you didn't know, takes intention, courage, and patience. Many of us are the first in our families to do things that were once out of reach: own a home, start a business, invest in stocks or retirement, even understand credit or savings. When you're the first, there's no blueprint to follow. You're figuring it out while carrying the weight of both survival and legacy.

I didn't come from a family where we talked about money in terms of growth or planning. We didn't discuss budgets, investments, or saving for the future. Bills got paid, sometimes barely, and if there was anything left over, it was spent quickly. The idea of wealth, of intentionally creating and protecting it, felt like a concept meant for someone else. It was a short and fiery young Staff Sergeant named Cox who shifted that for me. "Just open a Roth IRA," she said. "Put 5% of every check in there and watch it grow." She said it as if it were simple, but to me, at the time, it felt like a foreign language. She talked about emergency funds, and I nodded, not fully understanding. What was an emergency fund? How much should I have? What did I do with it? I was 21, and the idea of retirement and financial security felt so distant, so far removed from my daily reality. But I trusted her. I opened that account, not because I had it all figured out, but because something in me knew I had to start somewhere.

Over time, I continued to learn. I created an Excel template to track and project my savings. It was basic, but it helped me see my progress in a way that felt real. About ten years after opening that Roth IRA, I connected with a financial adviser who helped me understand the importance of life insurance, not just for myself, but also for my children. He taught me what a real emergency fund looked like: six months of living expenses, saved and untouched. I began budgeting for things I'd once thought were luxuries, like travel. I even set up brokerage accounts for my kids so they could start their lives with tools I never had. None of this knowledge was passed down to me. It wasn't inherited wisdom. I had to gather it piece by piece. My family knew how to spend, how to enjoy. But making your money work for you, creating something lasting, was knowledge I had to chase.

Still, every decision I made, every new term I learned, or account I opened felt like reclaiming something that should have always been mine. I wasn't just saving, I was rewriting the story. I was planting roots where there had only been survival. I was proving, to myself and to those watching, that financial wellness was not a privilege reserved for others. It's possible for us too. It belongs to us too.

So yes, this journey can be overwhelming, especially when you're doing it on your own. But each step, no matter how small, is a declaration: you deserve more than enough. You deserve options, and rest, and peace of mind. Your children deserve to inherit more than hustle and debt. They deserve freedom. This is not about greed. This is about healing the relationship between your worth and your wealth, knowing you are worthy of overflow, not just endurance. Most importantly, it's about understanding the wealth you build isn't just for you – it's a bridge. A path. A new beginning for generations to come.

Practical Ways to Begin Building Wealth:

Practical ways to begin building wealth are not just about numbers on a spreadsheet, they are about reclaiming agency over your life. For many of us, the very idea of financial education can feel triggering or even embarrassing. We were told to save but never shown how. We were told to work hard, but not how to make our money work for us. And when you've spent years just trying to make it day to day, the thought of planning decades ahead can feel both overwhelming and surreal. But starting where you are is enough. Financial education is not a race, it's a relationship, something you build over time one step, one decision, one resource at a time. There are free podcasts that explain credit in ways that feel honest and accessible. Books that speak directly to our experiences of growing up in households where the lights may have been turned off, but the desire to do better always burned quietly. You don't have to learn everything at once. But you do owe it to yourself to begin.

Entrepreneurship is more than a business; it's a form of freedom. Turning your ideas, creativity, and lived experiences into income is not selfish. It's strategic. You don't need a degree in business to start. What you need is belief in your voice, your vision, and your capacity to grow. Whether it's selling handmade products, launching a consulting service, or creating digital content, every offering becomes a bridge toward autonomy. The beauty is, you can start small. A few hours a week. A side hustle. A test run. You don't have to quit your job tomorrow. But you do get to explore what it means to own your work, your time, your value. You get to stop asking for a seat and instead build your own table.

Investing is another vital piece, one that many of us weren't exposed to early on. It often feels like a secret language reserved for people in boardrooms, but it belongs to us too. You don't have to wait until you're wealthy to invest. You become wealthy by starting. Employer retirement plans, Roth IRAs, high-yield savings accounts, and even micro-investing platforms that let you purchase fractional shares are tools within reach. Consistency matters more than the amount. Whether it's $25 or $200 a month, what matters is the habit, the intention, the mindset shift from "I'll never have enough" to "I'm building something." You may not see immediate results, but you are planting something that your future self and your children will one day be grateful for.

Estate planning may feel like a distant concern, but it is an act of radical care. Wills. Trusts. Beneficiaries. Life insurance. These are not just formalities for the wealthy. They are love letters to your future lineage. They ensure that what you've worked for, no matter how big or small, is passed on with clarity and purpose. It means the people you love won't have to struggle through loss and confusion. It means your intentions live on even when you're no longer here to speak to them aloud. It is one of the most deeply responsible, dignified things you can do, not just for yourself, but for everyone who comes after you.

Building wealth isn't about burnout or climbing someone else's ladder. It's about designing a life where financial stability is the floor, not the ceiling. A life where your children don't have to unlearn scarcity just to dream. A life where ease, not anxiety, shapes your choices. It is possible. And it starts with you. You don't have to be perfect. You just have to be willing. Willing to learn, to unlearn, to try, and to keep going. Wealth, in its truest form, is not just about money; it's about possibility. And you are allowed to build a life full of it.

Financial Healing

Before we can create new money realities, we must first confront the stories we've inherited. Many of us were raised on quiet rules that lived beneath the surface of our homes. We were taught not with financial literacy, but with emotional cues, tight shoulders when the bills came, tension at the grocery checkout, whispered arguments when something couldn't be afforded. We were taught money was something to fear, to chase, to never talk about too loudly. Phrases like "We don't talk about money," "There's never enough," "You must work twice as hard to get half as much," or "Money is evil" weren't just said, they were lived. These ideas settled into our nervous systems long before we knew how to budget or balance a checkbook.

Because we didn't choose those messages, we often don't notice when they become the filter through which we make every financial decision. We find ourselves overcompensating, taking on extra shifts, saying yes to burnout, undervaluing our work because somewhere deep down, we believe we have to prove we're worthy of having enough. Or we hesitate to ask for a raise, undercharge in our businesses, or feel embarrassed about wanting to earn more, because we've been taught desire itself makes us ungrateful. Sometimes we reach a moment of success only to self-sabotage, not because we don't want to thrive, but because thriving feels unfamiliar, uncomfortable, and unsafe.

Financial healing begins with recognizing this isn't your fault and it's not your forever. It's choosing to look at your money story without shame and ask, gently, "Where did I learn this, and does it still serve me?" It's essential to understand your worth has never been tied to your productivity or paycheck. You don't have to earn your right to rest, to feel secure, to imagine more for yourself than just survival. Financial healing is about releasing guilt, not only for what you didn't know but for the ways you coped when you didn't have the tools or support. It's about forgiving yourself and others, not to forget, but to unhook yourself from cycles you never agreed to continue.

Ask yourself: What memories shaped my view of money? What was modeled to me about giving, saving, and receiving? What did I internalize about success, struggle, and sacrifice? Whose voices still echo in my mind when I go to spend, save, or invest, and do I want those voices guiding my future?

Healing your relationship with money is a sacred reclamation. It's about choosing to make peace with numbers, not because they define you, but because they can reflect your values, boundaries, and vision. It's letting yourself feel joy instead of guilt when your bank account grows. It's choosing to be curious instead of ashamed. It's looking at your debt and saying, "This doesn't define me, but I do have the power to shift it." It's building financial practices that align with your life, your truth, not just what the world tells you, you should want.

This is not just about money. This is about self-trust, reclaiming agency. It's about creating lives where wealth isn't feared, but honored; where abundance isn't just financial, but also emotional and spiritual. When we unlearn scarcity and lean into worthiness, we become the turning point in our families. We become the ones who don't just make more, we teach more, model more, and pass on more than just survival.

Financial healing is a gradual, gentle, and courageous journey. However, it is also a transformative process that starts with a powerful decision: I deserve to have enough. I have the right to aspire for more. And I can flourish on my own terms.

Breaking Scarcity Mindsets

Scarcity says: "There's not enough." Abundance says: "There's more than enough, and I am worthy of receiving it." But here's the truth: many of us have lived with it silently. Scarcity doesn't just show up in our bank accounts. It lives in our nervous systems. It hides in the tightness of our chest when we check our balance. It whispers in the background when we hesitate to ask for a raise, decline an opportunity we believe we're not ready for, or feel guilt creeping in when we start to have more than those we love.

Scarcity is a trauma response, a quiet inheritance passed down through generations told they didn't belong in rooms where decisions were made. Through women who made miracles out of pennies but never had the luxury of dreaming past the end of the month. It's the echo of systemic exclusion and withheld access, proof many of us were never taught to see money as neutral or supportive. We were taught to fear its absence more than we were taught to embrace its potential. And yet, it's not permanent. Even when it's woven deep, scarcity can be unraveled. Slowly. Gently. With love. The first step is noticing the internal language we've normalized: thoughts like *"I'm bad with money," "It's too late for me to get it right,"* or *"I'll never have enough."* Those aren't just casual worries, they're inherited scripts, survival mechanisms, and learned fears pretending to be facts. And they deserve to be questioned.

To break the cycle, we must identify those thoughts as echoes of a past that doesn't define our future. Then we replace them with affirmations of abundance, not toxic positivity but grounded truths that say: *"I attract aligned opportunities." "I am capable of learning." "Overflow is possible for me, too."* We begin to build a new inner dialogue that honors our power, rather than erasing our past. Surrounding ourselves with examples of financial expansion becomes essential. Not just influencers or aspirational figures, but real-life people, especially Black women, who are building, growing, learning out loud, and holding space for wealth as a joyful, transparent, communal conversation. Money doesn't have to be taboo. It can be empowering. It can be spiritual. It can be a tool of transformation, not just a means of survival.

We practice gratitude, not to bypass our needs, but to stay rooted. Gratitude for what we have, for the knowledge we've gained, for every small decision that's moving us forward. And also gratitude for what's on its way, the opportunities that haven't arrived yet but will. For the wisdom we're still unfolding into. Gratitude becomes the soil, not the ceiling. You don't have to be rich to feel abundant. You don't need six figures in savings to claim you are safe and held. Sometimes, abundance is a deep exhale after paying a bill without fear. Sometimes it's a refrigerator full of groceries or the decision to rest without guilt. Sometimes it's knowing you don't need to prove your worth through hustle anymore. You just need to feel safe, sovereign, and supported. That's the kind of abundance that lasts. The kind that doesn't waver when circumstances shift. The kind that cannot be taken because it lives inside you, built not on fear, but on truth. And that truth is this: you are allowed to have more than enough. You are allowed to trust yourself with wealth. And you are allowed to heal what was never yours to carry in the first place.

Aligning Wealth with Purpose

Money without purpose becomes another source of stress. Money aligned with your values becomes liberation. Many of us learn the hard way, accumulating just enough to survive or push forward, only to feel depleted, unfulfilled, or disconnected when we fail to meet financial goals. When money has no purpose beyond paying bills or proving our worth, it becomes something we chase, fear, or avoid.

However, when it reflects who we truly are and what matters most to us, it becomes something entirely different. It becomes a tool not just for security but for rejuvenation and freedom. It allows you to fund your healing in ways your past may never have made room for. That might look like therapy you no longer postpone. Retreats or rest you don't feel the need to justify. Wellness practices that root you back in your body. It gives you space to stop surviving and start tending to your spirit. That is a kind of wealth too: being able to afford your wholeness. It allows you to support your family with open hands and a full heart.

You can give not out of fear or scarcity, but from a place of knowing you aren't sacrificing your own well-being to show up for theirs. You're able to offer support in ways that don't silence your own needs. You can break cycles of lack not just financially, but emotionally, by providing your children, siblings, or elders the kind of care that comes with dignity, not depletion. It gives you the power to give generously, without the undertone of obligation or fear of loss.

You can invest in others, in movements, in community, because you know there is more than enough. That generosity reflects your abundance and alignment, not something that leaves you feeling smaller or spent. It allows you to create unapologetically. To turn your ideas, your stories, your visions into something tangible.

Money aligned with purpose gives you the freedom to build beauty, to reclaim time, to pursue rest, not just when everything else is done, but because you believe it is essential to your being. It gives you the authority to say *"no"* to anything that dishonors your spirit. The job that keeps you in a box. The relationships that chip away at your peace. The obligations that were never yours to carry. And just as powerfully, it gives you the freedom to say *"yes"* to what expands you, whether that's taking a leap, saying yes to rest, or choosing a life path that may not make sense to others but feels undeniably right to you.

So, ask yourself: *What do I truly want money for?* Not the answer someone told you to give. Not the one that sounds responsible or practical. The real one. The answer that comes from your belly, your soul, your wildest knowing. *How can my financial goals reflect my values, my legacy, and my joy?* Let your story, not shame, shape your goals. Let them carry your dreams, your family's healing, and your future. *Who am I becoming as I build wealth, not just in my bank account, but in my mindset and relationships?* Because wealth isn't just what you accumulate, it's how you live, how you love, how you rest. It's how you show up for yourself and others when the world is watching, and when it isn't.

Let your money reflect your truth. Let it nourish you deeply. Let it bless others in a way that feels grounded and sacred. Let it be a source of possibility, not pressure. Let it be what freedom feels like in your hands, shaped by your own values, your own timing, your own power.

Consider what you've had to let go of to feel free. What relationships, identities, or beliefs did you outgrow even before you had words for the growing? Freedom often comes at a cost. What was yours? Now that you're reclaiming more space for yourself, what kind of freedom feels worth fighting for – not just externally, but within?

Chapter 9
SISTERHOOD AS SANCTUARY

"When Black women hold each other, we become unstoppable."

There is something sacred that happens when Black women gather. We don't need a stage, a spotlight, or permission, just a circle, a moment, a truth shared between breaths.

In a world demanding we perform strength at the expense of softness, sisterhood becomes our safest rebellion. It's not something performative; it's not curated, polished, or transactional. It's something ancestral, deeply ingrained in our DNA. A kind of invisible thread tying us to one another across space, circumstance, and time. When we gather, even in whispers, we restore what this world has tried to strip away: our humanity, our wholeness, our right to be held.

We hold each other with tenderness that doesn't diminish our power, honesty that doesn't feel like an attack but an invitation. We see each other, truly see, and in that seeing, we remember ourselves.

We speak each other's names when others mispronounce or erase them. We make room for the fullness of our being. In sisterhood, our names are not questioned or diminished; they are honored, spoken with reverence, even in correction. There is a knowing between us, a deep familiarity with what it costs to move through the world as both invisible and hyper-visible. That knowing creates safety.

We see the ache behind the smile, the brilliance beneath the silence. We recognize exhaustion masked as "I'm good." We feel the weight behind "I've got it." Because we've all said those things while quietly falling apart and so we respond without forcing vulnerability, just presence.

This is a tribute to the strength and healing that resides within sisterhood. It's about the kind of love that doesn't need to be earned. The kind of protection that doesn't ask questions. It is that unspoken agreement: I will stand for you, even when the world sits in judgment. I will lift you, not because you're weak, but because you deserve to rise with ease.

I've been fortunate to find many sister circles throughout my life, each one revealing different layers of what love, accountability, and belonging can look like. But there was one moment during my third year working in primary care that changed me at my core. Military medicine is not built for consistency; it's a revolving door of leadership, expectations, and demands. Commanders came and went so fast there was rarely time to build trust, let alone real structure. Staff morale suffered. We were expected to run efficiently while rarely being seen, heard, or valued. And I, like many others, was just surviving.

That's when I met Major Woodie. She had this country accent and a laugh that filled the hallway. She radiated joy but wasn't naïve. She knew exactly how the system worked and she still chose to lead with compassion. She deeply cared about her people. For me, it meant everything that she was a Black woman. There's something about being led by someone who not only understands your workload but also understands *you,* the layered exhaustion, the code-switching, and the pressure to be exceptional just to be accepted.

The way she carried herself was magnetic. She didn't just lead; she embodied leadership. She balanced patient care, back-to-back meetings, and team dynamics without ever seeming depleted. Observing her was akin to witnessing a world of possibilities. She didn't have to express her belief in me; she demonstrated it through her actions. She threw opportunities my way, and instead of drowning in them, I rose. She said, "I would never let you fail," and I believed her because everything about her conveyed sincerity.

That year changed me. Under her wing, I transitioned from a burnt-out provider into an empowered Officer in Charge. I stopped seeing my position as something to survive and started seeing myself as someone who could lead, shift, and influence. She didn't do it by handholding. She did it by trusting me by *seeing* me. The thing about real sisterhood is that it calls the best out of you, even when you've forgotten it's there. It was that unspoken, written-in-our-DNA kind of bond that rerouted my entire path. It reminded me I was never meant to carry it all alone, that there is no merit in struggling in silence, and rising doesn't require isolation. Because no woman heals alone, and no Black woman should ever be expected to carry the weight of the world in silence. In community, we get to be more than resilient; we get to be soft, nourished, and held.

Sisterhood is not always about quantity. Sometimes it's one woman, one soul who sees you and says, "You're not alone in this." Sometimes it's a group chat full of daily affirmations. Sometimes it's a monthly dinner, a standing phone call, or a circle of women you meet once and never forget. What matters is the *quality* of the connection. What matters is that it's real. We are not meant to heal in isolation. The world teaches competition, hierarchy, and individualism. Our healing is communal. We thrive when we're rooted in relationships that affirm our growth and development. In spaces where we can fall apart and be reminded that broken doesn't mean unworthy. In rooms where our softness is celebrated, not shamed.

So let this be a call back to your circle. Or an invitation to create one. You don't have to do this alone. You were never meant to. Let sisterhood hold you. Let it speak life over you. Let it challenge and cherish you in the same breath. Because when Black women come together, we don't just support each other, we *transform*.

The Power of Black Women Holding Space

There is something profoundly transformative about the way Black women hold space, not just for others, but for visions, movements, families, and futures. It isn't a role we always chose, but it's one we've mastered out of love, wisdom, and a deeply ingrained understanding that if we don't protect what's sacred, it doesn't always survive.

Holding space as a Black woman means we are often the ones who sense the energy of the room before a word is spoken. We anticipate needs, translate silence, and offer presence even when our own needs have gone unmet. Whether in the workplace, at home, or within our communities, we show up with a quiet authority that doesn't need to shout to be heard. Our leadership often lives between the lines, measured in what we prevent, nurture, and uplift.

In corporate America, we are more than a diversity box to check or an inspirational quote during Black History Month. We are culture-shapers, creative thinkers, and emotionally intelligent leaders. We are the ones who see the ripple effect of a decision not just on the numbers but on the people. We understand systems and spirit. We bring ideas ahead of their time because we've always had to imagine more than what was offered.

Our presence in these rooms is a force, not a favor. We bring a blend of innovation and intention that makes companies not just successful but sustainable. When we're at the table, accountability grows. Possibility expands. The conversation deepens. We challenge complacency. We humanize productivity and we do so while carrying the weight of being underestimated, misread, or tokenized and still, we deliver. Not to prove our worth, but because we know that legacy is built in the details.

At home, we are the foundation. We are the ones called when someone is sick, struggling, or simply seeking comfort. We plan birthdays and pay the bills, we pray over our children and make time to pursue our own dreams, all while managing loads of laundry and work calls. We listen when no one else does. We carry stories, recipes, remedies, and traditions. We do so while healing from what we were never taught but somehow expected to know and, in the community, we're the glue. We organize the drives, start the group chats, and check in on folks who've gone quiet. We hold space in living rooms, at beauty salons, on porches, and in protest lines. We are the ones who send the late-night "you good?" texts. The ones who sit in sacred silence when there are no words. We know holding space doesn't always mean saying the right thing; it means being present enough to let someone fall apart without rushing them to rebuild.

But holding space isn't just about others, it's about reclaiming it for ourselves. Too often, we are taught being strong means being selfless to the point of disappearance. But true strength is knowing when to say, *I need, too.* It's knowing our value isn't measured by how much we sacrifice, but by how deeply we are willing to honor our own voice. Creating space for ourselves, unapologetically, is an act of resistance and a radical declaration of worth.

When Black women hold space, we don't just keep things together. We elevate them. We restore integrity to the process. We infuse moments with meaning. We create environments where it is safe to be whole, where truth is welcome. Where softness is not mistaken for weakness, and vulnerability is not punished but protected.

We aren't asking for permission. We never were. We're reclaiming the sacred role of being seen, supported, and celebrated not just as caregivers and leaders, but as whole human beings. Black women bring rhythm, depth, discernment, and soul to every space we enter. That's not decoration. That's transformation.

Healing Through Community and Therapy

Healing is not always linear and rarely is it solo. It doesn't follow a neat timeline or arrive in polished, predictable steps. Sometimes it comes in waves: grief one day, clarity the next. Sometimes it looks like laughter breaking through in the middle of a hard conversation. Other times, it feels like stillness, like survival, like simply getting out of bed. Healing doesn't always look like progress, but it is. Choosing to stay present with your wounds instead of numbing them is healing. Choosing to reach out, to tell the truth, to try again, that's healing, too.

Many of us carry trauma that didn't begin with us. We were born into families and systems shaped by survival. We inherited silence wrapped in love. We were taught to endure before we were ever taught to feel. That generational grief, the kind that seeps into your bones without you knowing why, it doesn't just disappear. It lives in our need to always be "the strong one," in our fear of rest, in our discomfort with being cared for. Hyper-independence became a shield because we were told no one was coming to save us. But now, we get to choose differently.

Therapy is not weakness. It is power. It is a protest. It is the quiet, courageous act of saying, "I deserve to be whole." It is rewriting the story that says our pain must be hidden to protect others' comfort. Therapy is choosing to listen to the wounded parts of ourselves without shame. It is the refusal to pass down what was never ours to carry. Every time a Black woman sits in a therapist's office or joins a healing circle, she does the work of generations. She honors what her grandmothers couldn't say out loud. She gives her daughters, nieces, and godchildren a new blueprint for success.

Therapeutic and community support can take many shapes. It may be working with culturally competent therapists who see you not just as a diagnosis, but as a layered, brilliant human navigating the complexities of Black womanhood. It may look like sitting in a circle with other women who hold space for your tears, your joy, your rage, and your softness without asking you to shrink. It may mean seeking spiritual guidance, ancestral connection, or mentorship from someone who speaks your soul's language. Or it could simply be making space in your friendships for conversations that go deeper, where the masks come off and truth is welcome.

Healing in community doesn't require perfection, it requires presence. It's hearing another woman say, "Me too," and feeling your body exhale. It's realizing you're not crazy, not too sensitive, not alone. It's being mirrored by someone who sees your brilliance even when you forget it yourself. That kind of resonance, where another soul bears witness to your becoming, it doesn't just comfort. It transforms. It rewires the stories shame tried to root in us.

We are not meant to carry the weight of our healing alone. We are not intended to be silent warriors with full hearts and empty cups.

We are meant to be seen. To be held. To be reminded softness is not a flaw but a return to who we were before the world demanded our armor.

Healing is a return to the truth, to self, and to the community. In those sacred spaces, therapy rooms, living rooms, sister circles, or quiet car rides with a trusted friend, something powerful happens. We begin to believe we are worthy of peace; not just survival, not just coping, but deep, anchored, and liberating peace. So let yourself be seen. Let yourself be known. Let others walk beside you, not because you are weak but because healing was never meant to be a solitary path.

Releasing Competition

The world has often taught Black women to compete for space, respect, visibility, and love. We've been conditioned to believe there's only room for one of us in positions of power, in relationships, in the spotlight. Scarcity told us there's only space for one Black girl in the room, and if we didn't fight to claim it, we'd be overlooked, erased, or replaced. That belief was born out of real systems that kept us out, overlooked us, and rewarded assimilation over authenticity. It was handed down like a shield: protect yourself, compete, don't let your guard down, because the world won't give you anything twice. However, the burden of the shield can become tiring the longer it is held. It keeps us from seeing each other as sisters. It keeps us guarded and silent when we need softness and solidarity the most.

Comparison becomes a slow-burning ache. It convinces us someone else's joy is a threat to our own. It tricks us into collapsing when we should expand, withholding praise when we should be celebrating, and staying quiet when we should be clapping. It creates a false sense of scarcity, whispering that her win is my loss, that her beauty makes me invisible, that her voice cancels out my own. Over time, comparison breeds resentment, even isolation. It can make us distrustful, defensive, or feel as though we must perform perfectly just to be worthy of love, success, or a sense of belonging. The longer we stay in that mindset, the more we disconnect from our own unique brilliance. We begin to question our gifts, hustle for validation, and view ourselves through someone else's lens.

But sisterhood begins where competition ends. It starts the moment we reclaim our truth: Your success is not my failure. Your beauty does not cancel out mine. Your joy expands the possibility for all of us. That kind of clarity is liberating. When we release the need to compete, we create space to be ourselves fully, freely, and unapologetically. We begin to celebrate not just what others have achieved but also what their success means for the collective. We see proof of what's possible. We share resources and wisdom because we know there's enough to go around. We uplift each other in rooms where decisions are made. We speak each other's names when opportunities arise. We take care of each other, emotionally and spiritually, because we understand our connection is the source of our power, not a source of competition.

Releasing competition doesn't mean we lose our ambition. It means we align ambition with love, purpose, and community. It means we become women who can look each other in the eye, say, "I'm proud of you," and truly mean it. It means we make space for one another to grow, evolve, stumble, and rise again. When we root ourselves in collective abundance instead of individual survival, we become unstoppable. We begin to build tables where we're not just invited, but fully digested. We begin to model for the next generation what it looks like to rise together, without stepping on each other to get there.

The future we deserve isn't built on rivalry. It's built on reverence. Reverence for our individual journeys, for our shared history, and for the power we hold when we link arms instead of competing for scraps. We were never meant to fight each other for visibility; we were born to reflect light to one another. When we finally let go of the lies keeping us small and separate, we begin to create something much bigger than success. We create liberation. We create a legacy. We create a new world where Black women are free to be fully human, together.

Embracing Collective Liberation

Individual success is powerful. It affirms the sacrifices we've made, the barriers we've broken, and the moments we chose ourselves even when it was risky. It can feel like a comfort, a reward, a necessary milestone after years of pushing through systems not built for us. But collective liberation? That's transformational. It's not just about one of us crossing the finish line; it's about building a world where there are no finish lines, only expansive beginnings. When we center community in our healing and our goals, when we prioritize shared growth over singular advancement, we begin to ask deeper, more meaningful questions. How can I use my platform, privilege, or power to open doors for others? Who do I bring with me as I grow, not just in name, but in real, tangible opportunity? What does it look like to build systems of care, not just capital? Systems that nourish our wholeness, not just our resumes. Systems that honor our humanity, not just our hustle.

This is an invitation to dream beyond the solo win. To look past the gold stars and accolades and envision a future that reflects the sacred power of *us*. It is a reimagining of success that encompasses our unity, our recovery, and our legacy, all together. Imagine networks of Black women co-creating life on their own terms. Not scattered and struggling in silence but unified, supported, and seen. Picture us building empires rooted in integrity, raising children with intention, writing books reclaiming our narratives, and investing together, financially, emotionally, and spiritually. Imagine us praying together, celebrating together, grieving and healing together, resting without shame, laughing without restraint, and living without fear. This is not idealism; it is ancestral wisdom in action. It's a remembering of who we were before we were told we had to do it all alone.

It's a return to the front porch, where the wisdom of our foremothers was shared through ideas, problem-solving, and strengthening the bonds of family and community. Where women found safety in one another's presence, where storytelling passed down more than memory, it passed down resilience and love. And now, in this modern era, we carry that wisdom forward. We turn healing circles into sacred ground. We turn group chats into lifelines. We turn business meetings into affirmations and referrals. We lift each other up in rooms that weren't made for us and still find ways to bloom. Collective liberation is not a theory. It's a practice. It lives in the everyday choices we make to show up for one another, in the affirmations we speak in meetings, the job leads we pass along, the space we hold when someone is grieving, birthing, or transforming into something new. It lives in the choice to call instead of judge, to support instead of competing, to listen instead of dismissing.

When we embrace collective liberation, we create space for nuance, tenderness, and radical support. We affirm no one's light dims our own. Your rising lifts me too. It is the antidote to hyper-independence. It is the medicine for comparison. It is the future so many of our ancestors dreamed of but never got to see. We now become the vision they held close. We become the living evidence their sacrifices were not in vain. When we lean into collective liberation, we step into a world where no Black woman has to question her belonging, her brilliance, or her beauty. We create a culture where being held is normal, where sharing the table is expected, where success tastes sweeter because we taste it *together*. And in doing so, we don't just heal, we build. We rise. We remember. We reclaim. We begin again, as a collective, rooted in truth and reaching for liberation that holds us *all*.

Reflect on the women who have held you up, who've seen you, affirmed you, and made space for your healing. What have those relationships taught you about trust, reflection, and shared resilience? Are there places where your walls remain up, even among those who love you? What kind of sisterhood are you calling in now, and how are you preparing yourself to receive it?

Chapter 10
THE POWER OF SOLITUDE

There was a time when being alone felt like a form of abandonment. When the silence screamed, and stillness felt like a punishment. As women, we are so often surrounded by noise, expectations, obligations, and roles we didn't ask for but carry anyway. We've been conditioned to associate our worth with our availability, our usefulness, and our proximity to others. But solitude? Solitude is something few ever taught us to revere. Yet it is in solitude where I learned to come home to myself.

Solitude, when chosen with intention, becomes a gift. It is not the same as isolation, which is often born of neglect or disconnection.

Solitude is an offering, a return to the quiet corners of your soul that are rarely witnessed, even by you. It is the space where performance ends and presence begins. Where the mask can fall and the truth can rise.

In solitude, I learned to listen, not to the world, but to my own inner voice, the one drowned out by "should," silenced by survival, and buried beneath the noise of being everything to everyone. I had to separate myself from the distractions long enough to realize my intuition had been speaking all along. The more I listened, the more it revealed not only what I needed, but who I truly was.

Stillness became medicine. It became something I craved, rather than feared. I began to carve out moments where I wasn't responding to texts, meeting deadlines, or tending to someone else's emergency. In that stillness, my spirit began to exhale. I began to breathe more deeply, think more clearly, and feel more. I could hear the whispers of my ancestors. I could hear the voice of God. I could hear myself.

Learning to love my own company wasn't easy. There were days when the silence unearthed grief, loneliness, or parts of myself I'd long ignored. But I stayed. I didn't run from the discomfort. I let the tears fall. I let the memories come. With time, I realized solitude didn't make me lonely, it made me whole. It reminded me I am enough, even when no one is clapping and no one is watching.

Solitude became a place of restoration. A journey back to myself. A ritual of coming home. It is where my creativity bloomed, where my clarity sharpened, where my soul recharged. It was where I remembered who I was before the world told me who I had to be. Solitude taught me being alone doesn't mean being unloved. It means I trust myself enough to be with myself. It means I no longer need constant validation to feel worthy. It means I have nothing to prove and everything to feel.

So, if you find yourself in a season of solitude, don't rush to fill the space. Don't confuse it with punishment. Let it be a sanctuary. Let it be sacred. Because it is in the quiet moments you remember: you were never truly alone. You were always with yourself, and that has always been enough.

The Cultural Fear of Being Alone

The Cultural Fear of Being Alone is one of the heaviest inheritances many Black women carry. It lingers beneath our relationships, decisions, ambitions, and the silences we rarely get to speak out loud. We are taught early, both subtly and directly, that to be seen as valuable, we must be needed. That our worth is tied to our ability to show up for everyone else, and that being chosen by a partner, a job, or a community is the highest marker of success. When we find ourselves in moments of solitude, without a hand to hold or a role to play, many of us feel a creeping sense of failure. Not because we've actually failed, but because we've been conditioned to believe solitude equals rejection. That not being constantly in motion, constantly partnered, constantly serving, means we've somehow missed the mark.

This is the generational wound: a deep-rooted fear that if we are not proving ourselves in love, labor, service, or companionship, we are nothing. Solitude becomes suspect. Rest becomes guilt. And the quiet? The quiet starts to sound like shame. We wear the mask of the "strong, single Black woman" not just to survive but to avoid the stigma of being seen as unwanted, unworthy, or somehow broken. We fill our calendars, our arms, and our homes to avoid the mirror of loneliness. And in doing so, we often abandon ourselves. But what if being alone is not the same as being unloved? What if solitude is not exile but sanctuary? What if our time with ourselves is not a punishment to endure but a sacred opportunity to return to our truth? Reframing solitude requires us to confront the noise we've inherited. It asks us to peel back the layers of survival, to acknowledge the grief beneath our constant striving, and to realize self-worth does not require an audience.

Solitude, when honored, becomes an act of self-devotion. It's where we hear the voice of our spirit without interruption. It's where we discover that our dreams, our laughter, our joy, and our softness can bloom without anyone else's permission. It's where we recognize we are not waiting to be chosen, we are choosing ourselves. And that choice is divine.

This is the revolution: to sit in our own company and feel not panic, but peace. To know being alone does not mean we've been left behind. It means we are finally listening inward. We are honoring the girl inside us who was told love had to be earned through sacrifice. We are resting, not running. Releasing, not performing. Rooting, not reaching.

When we reclaim solitude as sacred, we loosen the grip of generational shame. We begin to understand our value is not up for debate. We are whole, even when no one else is watching. We are enough, even when no one else is needing. And we are loved, deeply and eternally, most importantly, by ourselves.

Let that be the new inheritance. Let that be the legacy we pass on. A lineage where Black women are free to choose solitude without fear. A future where aloneness is not our enemy, but a way we connect with our higher self.

Relearning Stillness in a World of Noise

Relearning Stillness in a World of Noise is an act of remembering who we are beneath the performance. It's not just about taking a break from technology; it's about reclaiming a part of ourselves that's been buried under the noise of demands, deadlines, group chats, obligations, and expectations. The constant hum of being connected to others, to work, to the world, creates a kind of disconnection from our own inner truth.

For Black women, especially, the emotional labor of being "on" is magnified. We show up for our families, our communities, our careers, our causes, and even our timelines, often without pause. We pour and pour, giving light in places that rarely ask if we're burning out in the process.

Digital overwhelm has a way of creeping in slowly. One scroll becomes a hundred. One notification becomes twenty. And somewhere amid all that noise, our own voice, the one that knows what we need, when we need rest, when we need quiet, when we've had enough, becomes muted and quiet. Until we forget how to hear it. Or worse, we begin to distrust it.

The impact goes deeper than we often name. It's not just fatigue, it's fragmentation. A sense of being everywhere but never fully present. Never fully grounded. Never fully with ourselves. In a culture that equates constant visibility with value, stillness becomes misunderstood. It's often confused with laziness, framed as non-productive, or viewed as a form of isolation. But stillness is not absence; it is presence. It is depth. It is a return. Stillness is where we remember we don't have to earn rest. Our existence is not validated through how much we produce or how quickly we respond. We don't have to perform strength to be worthy of softness. Stillness is where our body tells the truth, our words won't speak. It's where clarity rises from the quiet. And the longer we ignore the call to be still, the further we drift from our center.

Reclaiming stillness is a sacred rebellion in a world that demands we stay busy, accessible, and endlessly available. It doesn't require drastic change; it begins with small, intentional acts that whisper to the soul: "You deserve this." It might look like waking before the house stirs, just to be with your breath and a warm cup of tea or taking a silent walk without your phone. Saying no to one more obligation and yes to your peace. Setting boundaries with your time, your screen, and your energy. Choosing to log off, to go inward, to tend to your spirit without apology. Stillness is not detachment; it's a deeper connection. To yourself. To the divine. To the truth that cannot be heard through noise. And when we allow ourselves to sit in that stillness, really sit, we start to hear things we've long silenced: desires, needs, grief, dreams. The voice of our own becoming.

For Black women, reclaiming stillness is especially vital because we've been taught to run before we're ready, to serve before we're full, to be everything to everyone but ourselves. As a result, stillness becomes the medicine. The place where we remember we are not machines. We are not tasks to complete. We are whole beings with rhythms, seasons, and cycles. Let this be a sacred invitation to return to yourself. You don't have to post about it. You don't have to explain it. You don't have to earn it. Your stillness is not a luxury; it is your birthright. Let it be a sanctuary. Let it be your daily prayer. Let it be the space where you stop performing and start listening again. Inside the quiet, something sacred is waiting to rise and that something is you.

Solitude as Liberation from the "Caretaker Complex"

There is a quiet reality many Black women carry but rarely speak: the expectation to be everything for everyone. Not out of pride but because we were taught, directly or indirectly, our value lies in what we offer others. That being needed is equivalent to being loved. That love, in fact, must be earned through self-sacrifice.

The role of caretaker is deeply embedded in our cultural memory. Generations of women before us were expected to show up substantial, available, and endlessly giving, no matter the personal cost. We inherited that role without question. We learned to tend to others even when our own hearts were breaking. To be the emotional anchor in our families, our friendships, our communities, even when we are silently drifting. And when we tried to rest, we were met with guilt. When we chose ourselves, we questioned whether it was the right choice. Being centered in our own lives felt unfamiliar. Even selfish. That is the weight of the caretaker complex: not just the act of giving, but the internalized belief we are only as good as the emotional, physical, and spiritual labor we provide. It is the kind of conditioning that tells you rest is earned, that your grief must wait, and that joy must be tempered if others are still struggling. So many of us carry that silent burden, unsure how to put it down without feeling like we're abandoning someone. But solitude interrupts that cycle. It gives us permission to explore who we are outside of our service. It creates a space not just for rest, but for realignment. In solitude, we begin to separate what we do from who we are. We start to ask ourselves honest questions without the noise, without the demands, without the performative smiles. What do I need today, not as a nurturer, but as a human being? What emotions have I been suppressing to keep showing up for others? What would it mean to be fully present with myself?

Solitude is not a retreat from love; it's an invitation to experience it in its purest form, starting with oneself. It is not a rejection of community, but a rebalancing of priorities that have for too long placed us at the bottom of our own lists. It allows joy to emerge from within, not as a reaction to someone else's needs being met but because *your* soul is finally being heard. It makes room for grief as a necessary truth rather than something shameful. It creates space for curiosity about your desires, fears, boundaries, and becoming.

Choosing solitude is not the absence of care; it is care redirected. It is a sacred act of remembering your life is your own. That your worth is not contingent upon how well you hold others and your needs, emotions, and ease, are not optional. They're essential. In solitude, we discover we are not here only to carry. We are here to be witnessed, to feel deeply, to evolve. We are here to experience fullness, not just fulfill roles. And when we return to others from a place of self-knowing, we bring a deeper version of ourselves, one rooted not in duty, but in truth. This is the quiet, steady liberation that solitude offers. Not loud or dramatic. But deeply personal. And wholly yours.

Creative Expansion and Spiritual Downloads

Solitude, when we stop running from it and finally sit in its presence, becomes a wellspring. It is not isolation or punishment. It is presence. Intimacy with one's own breath, one's own thoughts, one's own spirit. I have learned that when I stop striving and performing, when I retreat from the endless doing that the world demands, something sacred begins to happen. Ideas come more easily. Clarity sharpens. My own voice, the one often drowned out by responsibilities, distractions, and noise, rises to the surface like truth breaking through still water. In solitude, I don't have to explain myself. I don't have to retract or stretch to meet anyone else's needs; I just *am*, and that is where the breakthroughs begin.

It was in those quiet, often uncomfortable moments, when the phone was off, the house was silent, and I had nowhere to run but inward, that I realized I'd been carrying creative gold inside me all along. The problem was, I'd been too busy to hear it. Too distracted to see it. I was giving my best energy to surviving and keeping up, not to listening and birthing what was uniquely mine. Solitude changed that. It taught me how to become a student of my own spirit. It revealed that when I allow divine flow to move through me, without rushing, questioning, or needing it to make sense to others, magic happens. Books are written. Visions are born. Whole new versions of myself are realized.

There is a sacred lineage of this kind of retreating. Our ancestors, especially our foremothers, understood solitude was something to be honored, not feared. They slipped away into the woods, the prayer closets, the quiet corners of their lives, not because they were hiding, but because they were listening. They knew wisdom doesn't always scream. Sometimes it hums gently in the background, waiting for us to be still enough to notice. The wilderness wasn't just about escape. It was a place of preparation, of spiritual download, of divine clarity. And we, as Black women, carry that same ancestral knowing in our bones.

Solitude is where I've learned to trust the whispers, the nudges that say, "apply anyway," "let that go," or "build it from scratch." It's where I've learned to stop doubting my own wisdom just because it doesn't echo the noise of the world. It's in those moments of stillness that I've written from my soul, built ideas into businesses, drawn boundaries that protect my peace, and prayed prayers that pulled me out of despair. Not because someone told me to. But because Spirit met me in the quiet and handed me back to myself. And this isn't just my story. I've seen Black women all around me return to themselves through solitude. I've seen women heal decades of inherited pain simply by getting still long enough to hear their own truth. I've witnessed them step into bold, creative visions after finally giving themselves permission to pause. I've seen them dream bigger, love deeper, walk away stronger, not because they had all the answers, but because they finally made space for them to arrive.

Solitude is not a void. It is a beginning. It's where our spiritual and creative revolutions take root. It's where we learn, maybe for the first time, that we do not need to be filled by the outside world to feel whole. We already are, and in that stillness, in that self-honoring pause, we return to the sacred rhythm of becoming. So, if the world tries to convince you that stillness is laziness, that quiet is a sign of emptiness, or that solitude is just a softer name for loneliness, I invite you to challenge those notions. What if solitude is your doorway to something divine? What if, in choosing to be alone, you are choosing to finally hear the wisdom that's been waiting for you? What if this silence is not the end, but the origin of everything new you're being called to birth? The visions, the books, the businesses, the boundaries, they don't come from the chaos. They rise from the quiet, and in that quiet, you rise too.

Reparenting the Inner Self in Solitude

Solitude became the place where I could finally meet myself fully, honestly, and without interruption. In the quiet, I didn't have to perform strength; I didn't have to manage anyone else's emotions. I could simply sit with my own and let them speak to me. Alone time created the emotional space I didn't know I needed; it allowed me to witness and soothe the little girl in me who still carried questions, pain, and the ache of what was never said aloud. My book, *Sixteen Years to Life*, was born from that sacred space. It came from the stretch of time in my life when both my mother and father were absent and I was left, at just eleven years old, to navigate the aching silence that followed. Being unseen, too young to make sense of what was happening, but old enough to feel the sharp sting of abandonment. The loss of love, acceptance, and security leaves a wound time alone does not always heal.

For years, I coped by staying busy. I poured myself into achievement; I took pride in being dependable; I carried other people's pain like it was mine to bear. That's how many of us survive, by staying in motion, by tending to everyone else so we don't have to confront the void inside ourselves. But solitude finally slowed me down. It peeled back the noise and distractions, leaving only truth and the version of me that had gone unseen for too long. In solitude, I stopped running. I turned inward. I sat with the grief I'd buried and the longing I'd ignored. I gave myself permission to return to the wounds, not to stay there, but to understand them, to reclaim the parts of myself I had abandoned.

I began writing love letters to myself. It felt awkward, unnatural even, but over time, it became a lifeline. I stood in front of the mirror and spoke affirmations aloud; my voice trembled at first, but I didn't turn away. "You are worthy." "You are not too much." "You are not invisible." With each word, I stitched a bit of myself back together. I revisited core memories, not to relive the pain but to extend the compassion I never received in those moments. I told my younger self, "You should never have had to carry that alone," and I meant it. I gave myself the comfort, protection, and encouragement I once desperately needed but never had.

Solitude became my sanctuary. It was a container where all of me could exist: grief, rage, joy, confusion, laughter, and tenderness. There was no one to perform for, no one to please, just me, with myself, learning how to be my own home. I stopped shaming myself for what I felt and started honoring what was asking to be healed. Slowly, I began to reparent the little girl in me. I held her through the hard days, celebrated her resilience, and reminded her she was never truly alone, even when no one showed up. I showed up. And in doing so, I shifted the foundation I stood on.

This work of reparenting, of healing from the inside out, is not just for me. It's for the woman I continue to become, the children I may raise, the partner I will one day love with clarity and wholeness. I want to offer love undistorted by unhealed trauma; I want to create safety that doesn't come at the cost of my own well-being. But before I could become that woman, I had to return to myself. I had to do the hard, beautiful, necessary work of becoming someone I could trust.

Solitude is not punishment; it is power. It is where we finally become the mother, father, friend, and guide we needed. It is where the healing begins, not with the expectation someone else will come to fix what's broken, but with the radical decision to love ourselves enough to do the mending. Alone, yes, but never abandoned. In solitude, we become whole. In that wholeness, we make space for a life no longer built on pain, but on the love we've finally learned to give ourselves.

Becoming Whole Without an Audience

Becoming whole without an audience is one of the most sacred and self-defining journeys I've ever taken. For so long, I measured my worth by how visible my progress was, how many people acknowledged my growth, how many "congratulations" I received, how many eyes were on me as I tried to become something more. It's easy to get caught up in that cycle when we're often taught our value is directly tied to how well we can perform, how strong, beautiful, or accomplished we appear in the eyes of others. But I learned, sometimes painfully, that transformation isn't always a shared experience. True growth often occurs behind closed doors, in quiet moments when no one is clapping and no one is watching. It happens in privacy, in the silence, when you choose yourself even though no one is there to applaud the decision.

Letting go of the need for someone to witness my transformation was a grieving process in itself. I had to mourn the version of me that longed for outside affirmation. I had to sit with the discomfort of being unseen and still know I mattered. Over time, a quiet, unshakable confidence replaced that longing. A rootedness. I began to trust my own reflection. I started to recognize the milestones no one else could see, the nights I held myself through anxiety, the mornings I got up when it felt impossible, the boundaries I held even when my voice trembled. Those invisible victories became more meaningful than any public recognition because they were mine alone.

Acknowledging my own personal success has allowed me to cultivate a deep internal knowing, one that doesn't need to be shouted from the rooftops. It's a confidence that whispers rather than roars. It grows every time I make a choice that honors my peace, every time I release the urge to explain myself, every time I pour back into myself without making a public statement about it. It's an integrity I carry within, one that doesn't shift depending on who is watching. And that kind of quiet power? It changes everything.

Choosing solitude, real solitude, isn't about turning away from the world. It's about turning toward yourself with intention. It's about reclaiming your voice when it's been drowned out by noise, expectations, and applause. It's about deciding your wholeness isn't something to be proved or performed but to be nurtured privately, fiercely, and consistently. When I began to redefine what it meant to be whole, I realized I didn't need to be chosen by someone else to be enough. I didn't need to be paired, praised, or partnered to feel valid. I began to understand my value was never up for debate; it was simply mine to reclaim.

To any woman reading this who feels unseen, I want you to know: your healing still counts. Your evolution is still real. Just because no one witnessed the breakdown doesn't mean your breakthrough isn't worthy. You don't need an audience to validate the work you're doing in your spirit. You don't need the world's applause to know you've arrived at something sacred. Your quiet choices matter. Your private healing matters. Your soft "yes" to yourself matters. There is profound tranquility during the quietly unfolding season of growth. There is liberation in no longer needing your transformation to be broadcast. Becoming whole without an audience is not about retreating; it's about choosing to be deeply rooted in who you are, regardless of who sees it. That kind of wholeness? It cannot be taken, shaken, or performed. It is yours. Always.

Choosing Solitude Without Shame

Choosing solitude without shame is one of the most personal and powerful decisions a woman can make. For too long, our lives have been framed by others' expectations, measured by how much we give, how available we are, how seamlessly we hold everything and everyone together. That script rarely leaves no room for our own tranquility, our own breath, our own evolution. And yet, choosing to be with ourselves, without apology or performance, is a declaration we are not defined by service, partnership, or productivity. It is an affirmation our presence, even when quiet, is valuable.

I've learned solitude is not a void to be filled with noise or validation; it is a space to hear what has long been silenced within. It is where I confronted not loneliness, but a longing to reconnect with parts of myself I'd neglected while tending to everything else. What began as a choice for peace soon became a necessity for survival. It became a space to ask better questions of myself: What do I want, not just what's expected of me? Where do I feel safe? What brings me joy, not just purpose?

Many of us carry an unspoken guilt when we step away from others' needs to tend to our own. That guilt can be inherited, shaped by generations of women who were never allowed to rest without being labeled selfish or ungrateful. But the truth is: peace is not something we owe an explanation for. We are not abandoning anyone by choosing ourselves; we are simply returning to the center we were never meant to leave behind.

Solitude is not lack; it is a gathering of self. In that gathering, we reclaim the attention that was once scattered. We remember our worth is not tied to how much we're seen, chosen, or consumed. We begin to live in alignment with a more grounded truth: we matter even during loneliness. We are enough even in silence. When you embrace solitude, you start to see yourself not as an afterthought, but as your own sanctuary. You start to make room for your own energy before giving it away. And from that place of rootedness, your life begins to shift, not because someone applauds your growth, but because you finally believe you deserve to thrive without needing an audience to validate it.

The mental benefits are subtle but transformative: greater clarity, deeper boundaries, and emotional resilience. Physically, you begin to recognize your body's rhythm without rushing to meet someone else's. Spiritually, there's space to connect with your own wisdom, not just the voices around you. Emotionally, solitude becomes a mirror: not one that judges, but one that invites you to see yourself with compassion.

This is not about isolation, it's about sovereignty, knowing you're allowed to exist fully and freely, even when no one is watching. Your joy, rest, and quiet rituals are sacred – not because someone else approves, but because you finally do.

Reflection

Sit with your own presence. When you're alone, what surfaces? Is solitude a space for stillness or discomfort? Think about what being alone has taught you, what you've discovered about yourself when the noise quiets and the mirrors of others fall away. What truths emerge in the stillness that you've been too busy to hear?

Chapter 11
THE BODY REMEMBERS, THE BODY RECLAIMS

Our bodies are not separate from our stories. They carry what we forget, suppress, or silence. The body reveals what the mind denies. For Black women, this remembering is layered and ancestral. It holds unspoken grief, the tension of bracing ourselves to move through a world that misreads our existence, and the exhaustion of generations who had to push past pain just to survive. We are taught early to disconnect. To suppress the tremble in our voice. To stuff down the tears. To override the signals telling us we're not okay. We're taught to perform resilience like it's a badge of honor. To smile through heartbreak. To silence our grief in favor of grace. And in that performance, we begin to disappear from ourselves. We praise our strength, even when it costs us everything. We wear our endurance like armor, but inside, we are often bleeding, aching, unraveling slowly in places no one can see.

We begin to ignore the quiet cries of our own bodies: the pounding heart we dismiss as stress, the migraines we explain away as hormones, the back pain we blame on posture, the sleepless nights we chalk up to overthinking. But these aren't random ailments. They are signals, stories. They are the unspoken chapters our minds won't let us read but our bodies can't help but write. We've learned to treat our bodies as burdens or battlegrounds, tools to be disciplined, shaped, and controlled. Vessels that exist to work, to produce, to please. We're conditioned to see our worth through how much we can endure, not how well we are nourished. But our bodies were never meant to be sites of punishment or proving. They are sacred. Not because of how they look or how much they can bear, but because they are ours. Because they hold the breath of our ancestors, the rhythm of our lives, the truth of our becoming.

The body is more than bone and muscle. It is where our spirit resides. It is where our knowing lives. Where intuition whispers when the world gets too loud. It is the place where joy dances, where grief finds its voice, where softness waits patiently to be invited back in. And just as the body remembers harm, it also remembers safety. It can remember the feeling of being held. It can remember laughter, lightness, the kind of peace that doesn't ask for permission. But first, we must come home to it.

This chapter is an invitation to do just that, to return to your body not with fear or shame, but with reverence. To listen before pushing to honor before fixing. To relearn your body not as a problem to solve but as a partner in your healing. We will explore how movement, rest, breathwork, and body attunement can become pathways back to wholeness. We will reclaim the body not only as a witness to our pain but as a source of wisdom, freedom, and restoration. When we finally stop running from our bodies and start listening to them, we don't just heal – we remember who we were before the world told us to forget.

Embodied Trauma and the Journey Back In

Trauma often manifests in the body long before we have the language to name it. A racing heart. Shallow breath. Sleepless nights. Numbness. Hypervigilance. These are not signs of weakness or failure; they are intelligent, protective responses. The body, in its wisdom, remembers what the mind tries to forget. It adapts to threat even when we pretend we're okay. And when we experience ongoing stress or trauma, especially from a young age, the nervous system learns to stay on alert. It doesn't know how to turn off. Even when we're technically safe, our body behaves as if danger is right around the corner.

This is what nervous system dysregulation looks like. It's living in a state of chronic activation, where rest feels unsafe and calm feels like a lie. It's struggling to sleep because the mind won't stop racing. It's tight shoulders, feeling lightheaded when overwhelmed, and stomach pain no doctor can explain. It's reacting to minor stressors with big emotions. It's shutdown and numbness, followed by irritation and depression. It's being exhausted all the time, but never truly resting. And for many Black women, it becomes the norm. We learn to call it strong. We learn to call it resilience. We wear our exhaustion like armor.

I didn't have the words for this at the time, but by my 21st year in the military, I was living in that state of dysregulation, in survival mode without realizing it. I woke up tired. I pushed through body aches that lingered for weeks. I couldn't understand why I tossed and turned at night, why I always felt like I was running out of time, even when nothing was urgent. I was supplementing vitamin D, eating clean, and working out regularly, yet I kept gaining weight. I felt like I was fading from the inside out. The circles under my eyes darkened, my skin lost its glow, and my energy barely stretched far enough to get me through the day. No amount of willpower or wellness hacks could fix what my nervous system had internalized: constant stress had become my baseline.

It wasn't until I relocated to a less pressurized environment that I noticed a shift. The weekend work disappeared. My calendar opened up. I had space to breathe, really breathe. And slowly, my body began to exhale with me. My thoughts became less urgent. My sleep deepened. My skin regained color, and for the first time in years, I didn't feel like I was dragging myself through each day. This wasn't because I discovered some new supplement or trendy diet – it was because I finally removed myself from the conditions that kept my body in a chronic state of alert. What I needed wasn't more effort. I needed safety. I needed softness. I needed nervous system repair.

Healing begins when we listen deeply, not just to the thoughts in our head but to the cues and cries of the body. When we stop asking it to perform and start asking what it needs, that might mean sleep, or hydration, or gentle movement reconnecting us to our breath. It might mean saying no without guilt. It might mean crying without explaining. It might mean dancing, laughing, or lying still and doing absolutely nothing. The body will tell us. The nervous system will begin to settle when we create consistent cues of safety through ritual, rest, and nourishing relationships.

For Black women, this kind of reconnection is not just self-care. It is a revolutionary act. We were conditioned to suppress and endure, to keep moving no matter what. But we were never meant to live severed from our own bodies. We were never meant to confuse stillness with laziness or presence with weakness. Our bodies are not machines. They are sacred vessels of memory, intuition, and wisdom. We were not born just to survive. We were born to feel, to thrive. To be witnessed in our fullness, not just our function. Our healing is not optional; it's foundational. It is not a reward for hard work; it is fundamental. And the journey back into the body, the journey of finally saying, "I deserve to feel safe here," is one of the most powerful homecomings we can give ourselves.

Illness, Burnout, and the Urgency to Slow Down

There is a kind of weariness sleep does not fix, a fatigue that settles into the bones, into the breath, into the edges of who we are. For Black women, this is not simply exhaustion; it is the slow wear of a lifetime of overextension. We carry invisible but heavy responsibilities: managing households, showing up in the workplace, being emotionally available to everyone around us. And while the world often applauds our resilience, it rarely pauses to ask what resilience costs us.

Over time, the body begins to reflect what the spirit has been enduring. Autoimmune conditions, fibroids, chronic fatigue, high cortisol levels, anxiety, and panic disorders are not isolated medical phenomena. They are the cumulative result of running on empty for too long, of living in a state of constant output without replenishment. These conditions disproportionately affect Black women not because we're inherently predisposed to illness but because we are so often positioned to care for others at the expense of ourselves.

We are not machines. We are not meant to override our bodies to meet unrealistic expectations. Illness is not a punishment. It is not weakness. It is the body's intelligence stepping in when we have gone too far for too long. It is a signal our current way of living isn't working. And yet, many of us keep pushing, masking symptoms with caffeine, silencing pain with over-the-counter pills, and suppressing the anxiety keeping us wired and restless in the name of being "strong." This pattern of over functioning is unsustainable. It chips away at our physical vitality and emotional clarity, leaving us feeling like shadows of ourselves.

The urgency to slow down is not optional; it is a survival strategy. It is a conscious choice to stop living on autopilot and begin creating lives rooted in care and intention. Slowing down doesn't mean giving up on ambition. It means realigning your pace with your capacity. It means choosing to listen to your body when it whispers rather than waiting for it to scream. It means getting honest about what your nervous system can handle, about how overstimulation and chronic stress have become normalized, and how dysregulation has been mistaken for drive.

To restore balance, we must begin to identify the habits and environments that perpetuate cycles of fight, flight, or freeze. The hypervigilance many of us have lived with for years is not our natural state but rather a response to prolonged stress and a lack of safety. When we slow down, we give our nervous systems a chance to return to a state of equilibrium. We begin to recognize what calm feels like. This is not just about stress reduction; it's about cellular healing, hormonal regulation, and restoring a sense of embodied wholeness burnout and illness have stripped away.

Slowing down is not an absence of movement; it is a shift in direction. It is asking, "What does my body need to feel whole today?" instead of "What do I need to do to be enough today?" It is checking in before checking out. It is choosing nourishment over numbing, reflection over reaction, and presence over performance. As we begin to honor our limits, we discover new capacities, space for creativity, clarity, and deeper self-awareness. Slowing down opens the door to self-trust. It teaches us we don't need to earn rest or prove our worth through burnout. We are worthy *now*. We are allowed to rest *now*. Our healing does not require permission.

Let this be the season where we no longer negotiate with our well-being or wait for a crisis to make a change. Let this be the season where we slow down, not because we've hit a wall, but because we choose to listen, to honor, and to finally come home to ourselves.

Movement as Memory, Movement as Medicine

Movement becomes a medicine, not a punishment. Stretching, dancing, walking, not for weight loss or aesthetics but for liberation. To feel the body from the inside out, to reconnect with the wisdom it holds. For too long, movement has been framed as a task, something we do to fix ourselves, shrink ourselves, mold ourselves into something more acceptable or more desired. Many of us inherited this narrative: our bodies are projects in need of constant improvement and movement must be earned or endured. But there is another way to move, one centering care, presence, and intention. One that reminds us that our bodies are not problems to solve but homes to live in.

When I began to unlearn the punitive relationship I had with exercise, I found myself craving movement that felt gentle, intuitive, and alive. Not forced. Not aggressive. I found healing in slow, deliberate stretches that opened places I hadn't touched in years, in hips that held grief and shoulders that carried invisible weight. I found comfort in walking without a destination, letting my body set the pace. I found joy again in dancing in my living room, eyes closed, bare feet grounded in my own rhythm. These moments were not about burning calories; they were about returning to myself.

Rest is a form of resistance, yes, but movement can be too. Restful movement exists outside the hustle culture mindset. It invites us to move not to chase a goal but to release what lingers, to circulate what has been stagnant. When we move with intention, with breath and care, we signal to the nervous system it is safe to soften. We no longer have to brace or prove. We are simply allowed to be.

There is a quiet power in this kind of movement. It brings us back into a relationship with our bodies on our own terms. It asks us to be curious rather than critical. To ask: What do I need today? What would feel good, not look good? Maybe it's lying on the floor and breathing into tight spaces. Maybe it's standing in the sunlight and swaying to music that moves the soul. Maybe it's a slow, steady walk under the sky, not for steps or tracking but for peace. Movement becomes prayer. Movement becomes presence. This shift toward intentional, restorative movement helped me begin listening more closely to my body's signals. Not just the big cries for rest but the subtle whispers, the tightening of the chest, the weight in my legs, the shallowness of breath. I started to respond, not ignore. To slow down, not override. This practice of listening changed everything. I began feeding my body when it was hungry instead of waiting until it was empty. I learned to stop when I felt tired, not when the work was done. I moved to feel, not to perform. In doing so, I reclaimed something no one ever gave me permission to have: agency over my own body.

For Black women especially, this reclamation is sacred. We live in a society that has long exploited our bodies, silenced our needs, and disregarded our pain. To return to our bodies with tenderness, to move from a place of care rather than correction, is an act of radical self-regard. Movement then becomes a bridge back to ourselves. A place where memory lives, where pain is metabolized, and where joy can return. Movement as medicine reminds us healing doesn't always happen in stillness. Sometimes it happens when we give ourselves the freedom to flow, gently, intentionally, and without shame. When we let our bodies lead, we begin to repair the trust that was lost. We come home to ourselves, not as objects to fix but as living, breathing, feeling beings worthy of love and presence.

This is the invitation: move in ways that make you feel alive, held, and whole. Not because you have to, but because you get to. Your body is a vessel of wisdom, not a battleground. When you listen, it will show you the way back to yourself.

Reclaiming Pleasure and Presence

So many Black women have lived their lives in survival mode. We know how to endure, hustle, and keep going no matter what. But few of us were taught how to feel good simply because we deserve to. Not because we earned it, not because we completed the checklist, but because we are entitled to presence and pleasure.

This was not a lesson we inherited. Our lineage is rich with resilience, but often at the expense. We inherited the strength to push through but rarely the permission to soften. As a result, many of us learned to associate pleasure with guilt, irresponsibility, and distraction. We learned to delay joy until the work was done, until the pain passed, until everything and everyone else was okay. In doing so, we placed our own aliveness at the bottom of our list.

Pleasure is not just sexual, it's sensory, emotional, and spiritual. It's found in deep breaths, in laughter, in music that moves through your chest. It's in taking your time with a meal, in moisturizing your skin slowly, in choosing clothes that feel like joy. It's in giving yourself permission to enjoy a moment without needing to justify it. It's in the morning light on your face, in hearing your own voice sing in the kitchen, in sipping tea without multitasking. It's found in the sacred pause between doing and being, when we allow ourselves to receive, without shame, without apology.

Pleasure serves as a reminder that our existence is not solely about enduring challenges; we are here to feel not just the weight of pain, but the lightness of contentment, the richness of being alive. Reclaiming pleasure is about rewriting the script that said we had to earn it. You don't have to prove your worthiness. It's already yours. Pleasure is not a reward. It is a resource. A compass. And presence with your body, your breath, your emotions is just as sacred. In a world that constantly pulls us out of ourselves, choosing to be fully in your body, right now, is essential. Presence enables us to recognize the underlying truth behind our actions. It's what helps us hear the whisper of our own needs before they become screams. Checking in with your breath, sitting in silence without reaching for distraction, being with yourself in stillness is not avoidance. It is an embodiment.

Presence with self is about honest connection rather than perfect mindfulness. It's allowing your thoughts to rise without judgment, giving space to your feelings without needing to fix them. It's about grounding yourself in the moment, rather than dwelling on the past or worrying about the future. It's pausing long enough to ask yourself, "What do I need?" and trusting your answer is worthy. To honor your physical self beyond endurance is to make a declaration: I am more than what I've survived. I deserve to feel alive, not just in the aftermath of pain, but in the fullness of life.

When you give yourself permission to prioritize pleasure and presence, you shift the paradigm. You teach your nervous system safety can exist without hypervigilance. You show your spirit peace doesn't have to wait. You reclaim your time, not just on the clock, but in the intimate, internal sense of belonging to yourself. This is how we begin to live. Not from urgency, not from performance, but from truth. From joy. From the fullness of being human.

From Survival to Sovereignty

This is about more than healing. It's about no longer asking your body to prove its worth. It's about releasing the guilt around care, the shame around pleasure, and the fear of slowing down. It's about knowing your body is your ally. Your witness.

For so long, survival meant being efficient, measured by output, and admired for what one could accomplish. But sovereignty requires a different kind of presence. It calls you to consider how much of your life has been shaped by urgency, and how many decisions were made not out of desire but out of necessity. It asks you to notice what you've postponed for later: contentment, stillness, and trust in your own rhythm. Later may never arrive unless you reclaim it now.

Sovereignty is not just a concept; it is a lived choice. It is the refusal to operate from a position of depletion. It is a personal standard where the bare minimum is no longer enough, where care is no longer delayed until collapse. It is learning to pause without guilt and give yourself what you've always needed without waiting for permission or consensus. For many Black women, choosing to center your well-being in a world that constantly demands your detachment from it is subtle but radical.

When a Black woman remembers her body, she reclaims her power. Not in a performance or a moment of external validation, but in her quiet decisions, how she prepares her mornings, the limits she now honors, the way she speaks to herself when no one is watching. She recognizes she no longer has to earn her own tenderness. She can belong to herself without needing to be useful to everyone else. When she listens, she heals. And that healing doesn't always come in grand breakthroughs. Sometimes it arrives in small recalibrations, in the decision to sit for a moment longer, to respond later, to ask herself what she wants before answering someone else. These moments become the ground on which her sovereignty is built. Not rushed, not forced, but nurtured by her willingness to stop pretending she's fine when she isn't.

When she honors, she liberates. She stops negotiating with exhaustion. She no longer waits for a crisis to make herself a priority. She learns to access her own clarity, not in isolation from the world, but in her ability to remain whole inside of it. Her energy becomes less reactive, more intentional. Her "yes" carries weight. Her "no" is no longer softened for comfort. In liberation, she writes a new story rooted in alignment, rather than performance. A story where her needs are no longer framed as burdens but as indicators of aliveness. A story where she creates time for a joy that isn't earned through suffering, where her capacity expands not through pressure, but through balance. Sovereignty is her ability to stand in her fullness, not just as someone who has healed, but as someone who now chooses how she lives, how she gives, how she receives.

This isn't about arriving. It's about staying present with yourself long enough to know what you need and trusting you are allowed to give it to yourself. It's about becoming the kind of woman whose care for herself is not reactionary; it's routine. Whose boundaries aren't negotiable, they're nonverbal agreements with her own peace. Sovereignty isn't loud or polished. It is practiced daily, even in the quietest parts of your life. And once you taste it, you realize there is no version of you more powerful than the one who chooses herself – deliberately, unapologetically, and without delay.

Reflect on the ways your body has carried your story, your joy, your grief, your survival. Where does it ache? Where does it resist? Where does it soften? Think about how your body has protected you, and how it may now be asking for a different kind of relationship. What does it look like to listen, to honor, to reconnect?

Chapter 12
UNLEARNING SILENCE

There comes a point in every Black woman's life when she realizes the silence she once used to survive now suffocates her. It creeps in quietly, disguised as grace, composure, resilience. It shows up in the pause before saying what you really mean, in the way your voice softens when it wants to roar, in the way you apologize for your tone, your truth, your very presence, even when you've done absolutely nothing wrong. At first, it feels like wisdom. Like self-preservation. Like knowing how to read a room, how to bite your tongue before your words cost you your job, your peace, your belonging. But over time, that silence becomes heavy. Thick. Unbearable. Not because we don't know how to hold it, but because we've held it for far too long.

We were taught early that survival depended on our silence. That "being a good girl" meant being agreeable. That "being strong" meant not breaking, even when we were already broken. We learned to adjust ourselves, edit our emotions, and speak just enough but never too much. So many of us grew up speaking half-truths and wearing whole masks, not out of dishonesty but out of necessity, because the world didn't make room for our full expression. Our pain made others uncomfortable. Our anger was weaponized. Our joy, when too loud, was mistaken for arrogance.

Silence became our armor. Our inheritance. A learned language passed down from mothers and grandmothers who carried grief in their backs and wisdom in their eyes, women who didn't always have the luxury of softness or the space to fall apart. Their silence wasn't a sign of weakness; rather, it was a calculated strategy. It was the only means they had to safeguard themselves and their families. Therefore, we pay tribute to them. But we also must name the cost of silence. The cost of silence is genuine and far-reaching. It affects not only our inner selves but also our physical health, breathing, and relationships. We feel the heaviness in our chests when we fail to express ourselves, and the tightness in our jaws from suppressing truths we never articulated. There's a weariness in striving to be agreeable, in reshaping our identities for clarity, and in witnessing our words being rephrased, reframed, and repackaged by those who never had to hold back their voices to be acknowledged.

It's a quiet grief, the kind that doesn't always have a name. You start to feel the gap between who you've become and who you really are. You start to feel the emptiness created by all the words left unspoken and the parts of yourself you sacrificed to maintain harmony. For a time, perhaps that peace felt valuable. However, in the end, the price becomes too steep. Eventually, you can't unhear the sound of your own silence because we were never meant to live muted. We were never created to fit inside someone else's version of "acceptable." We are not here to shrink or contort ourselves for anyone's comfort. We are not here to survive the silence; we are here to break it. And when we finally do, when we begin to speak the truths we were once punished for, to honor the emotions we were told were too much, to reclaim the voice we were conditioned to believe was too loud, we don't just liberate ourselves. We liberate generations. We change the story. We give our daughters and our younger selves permission to show up whole, unapologetic, and unedited.

Unlearning silence is not just about making noise. It's about returning to the clarity we were born with, the clarity that told us when something didn't feel right, that nudged us to speak up before we were taught to suppress that instinct. It's about no longer second-guessing our lived experience just because someone else doesn't want to hear it. It's about refusing to abandon ourselves to make others comfortable. Our voices are sacred. Our truth is medicine. Our full presence is not a problem to solve; it's a gift to be witnessed. We are allowed to speak.

We are allowed to feel. We are allowed to be. And we don't owe the world an apology for taking up space.

The Echo of Inherited Hush

We inherit more than eye color and cheekbones. We inherit the way our mothers swallowed their feelings. We inherit the prolonged silences around the dinner table, the forced smiles, and the fleeting glances that conveyed more than words ever could. We carry forward the stillness, the careful self-control, the evasion of difficult discussions, and the silence that became instinctive. This was their method of shielding us. This was their means of safeguarding themselves.

The silence was not a coincidence; it was intentional. It emerged from centuries of observation, resilience, and endurance. For numerous mothers and grandmothers, maintaining silence was not just anticipated, but also crucial. To stay alive. To keep a job. To avoid punishment. To not be labeled angry, disruptive, or ungrateful. They lived in systems that punished truth, that pathologized emotion, that erased softness unless it was serviceable to someone else. Speaking freely came with consequences they could not afford to pay. So, they found ways to hold it in. And they taught us, directly or indirectly, to do the same. We watched them show up for everyone but themselves. We watched them choke down disappointment, apologize first, and smooth things over. We saw how they sacrificed voice for peace, their identity for approval, and their needs for survival. We didn't just learn silence, we absorbed it. That silence shows up in us. In the way we hesitate before sharing too much. In the way we edit ourselves in rooms that never saw us as whole to begin with. In the way we ask for help only after we've broken. The inheritance is quiet, but powerful. It becomes a reflex. It shapes how we love, how we fight, how we grieve. How we disappear even while we're right in the middle of a room.

Inherited silence was once a brilliant adaptation. It helped our people survive in cruel, dehumanizing environments. Our foremothers knew how to say just enough. They knew when to nod and when to stay silent. They didn't lack emotion. They just knew the world had no room for their rage, no tenderness for their pain. Their silence was not a sign of weakness; it was a kind of wisdom, an embodied understanding that some things could not be said safely. So, we honor that. We don't look back with blame. We look back with reverence and with clarity. Honoring them means we understand the conditions they faced. To honor ourselves means we must also ask: where has this silence outlived its purpose? Where does it now limit, instead of protect? What do we lose when we continue to carry it unexamined?

Emotional inheritance is complex. It's the tenderness we learned through observation. It's the stoicism we modeled before we knew what feelings were. And it's the ache that surfaces when our own voice gets caught in our throat, not because we don't know what to say, but because somewhere inside, we were taught it's safer not to say it. Breaking this cycle is not an act of rebellion against our lineage; it is an act of responsibility to it. It's saying: *Thank you for what you endured. Thank you for surviving. And now, I will choose differently so I can live a fully engaged life.* It's understanding silence once kept us alive but now expression will help us heal. To speak our truths, to feel without shame, to name what hurt and what still does: this is not about rejection. It is about expansion. We are allowed to do more than survive. We are allowed to ask new questions, write new endings, and give our daughters and ourselves a new starting point. The hush may still echo, but now, we get to decide what follows it.

The Cost of Dimming Your Light

There is a cost to constantly shrinking yourself to fit into spaces never built with you in mind. A quiet, corrosive toll that builds over time. It shows up in the way you second-guess your brilliance. In the way you soften your truth until it no longer sounds like you. In the way you rehearse your words so carefully, you forget what you actually believe. The world teaches us early that to be accepted, we must be agreeable. To be safe, we must be silent. To be loved, we must be easy to digest. However, the cost of being agreeable is quite high.

Playing small may feel like protection at first but over time, it becomes a slow death of self. The more we silence ourselves to keep the peace, the more disconnected we become from our own inner knowing. Confidence begins to wither. Clarity dims. And authenticity, once alive in us like breath, starts to feel like a risk we can't afford to take. We say less. We show less. We become careful, curated versions of ourselves, constantly managing perception instead of standing in our truth.

That performance is exhausting. And beneath it, resentment quietly grows – toward the people who expect our silence, the systems that reward our compliance. But mostly, toward ourselves, for all the moments we didn't say what needed to be said, where we chose peace over truth and disappeared in the process. That self-abandonment becomes a pattern that fractures our sense of wholeness, blurs our sense of self, and leaves us wondering who we even are underneath the layers we've learned to perform.

Spiritually, the cost is even greater. When we deny our full expression, we disconnect from our essence. We start living from the outside in, shaped more by others' expectations than our own truth. We lose touch with joy. With conviction. With that grounded sense of "I know who I am." The fragmentation intensifies, leaving behind a sense of burnout. This exhaustion stems not only from taking on too much but also from feeling inadequate in meeting our own needs throughout the journey.

At what point does survival become a form of self-betrayal? At what point does making yourself small to make others comfortable start to feel like disappearing? When we downplay our brilliance to gain acceptance, we convey a message to ourselves that we are excessive. That our voice, our needs, and our presence must be negotiated down. But the truth is: what the world calls "too much" is often just a woman in her fullness. A woman no longer willing to contort herself for proximity, approval, or peace at the expense of her soul.

You don't owe anyone your silence. You don't owe the world a smaller version of yourself to be worthy of belonging. The light in you is not the problem. The problem is a world that never learned how to receive it without feeling threatened. The cost of dimming your light is far too high. And you deserve to shine without apology.

The Language of Suppression

We were taught early that how we sound could either open doors or close them. Our voice, tone, pitch, and inflection could either invite respect or rejection. So many of us learned to master the unspoken rules. Code-switching became not a skill but rather a necessity. We learned to flatten our accents in professional settings. To avoid sounding "too Black" or "too emotional." We were taught to intellectualize our pain, to frame our truth in a way palatable to those who might otherwise dismiss it.

We did this not because we were ashamed of who we were, but because we were told survival depended on it. So we adapted. We edited our voices until they sounded like something someone else could understand. We buried the parts of our dialect that felt too raw, too real, too loud, too *us*. However, suppression comes with a price.

There is a sense of sorrow in being unable to express yourself authentically. A deep ache comes from having to filter your expression through someone else's comfort. Over time, it teaches you your natural voice is not good enough. That your native rhythm, your emotion, your cultural nuance must be translated, tamed, or toned down to be seen as intellectual, professional, or "articulate." It is a lie we are forced to perform to access opportunity, one that fractures the authenticity of our communication and chips away at our sense of self.

Being told you "talk white" becomes less of a compliment and more of a wound. Being told you "sound ghetto" becomes a coded insult meant to silence. Even being told you're "so well spoken" becomes less about your ability to express and more about others' surprise that you are intelligent *despite* sounding like you do. But we do not need to perform whiteness to be worthy. We do not need to hide our vernacular to be valid. Our language, our slang, our drawls, our storytelling, is a living, breathing archive of our culture. It holds our survival, our creativity, our intimacy, our fire. It is not less than; it is layered, complex, and beautiful.

Dismantling linguistic respectability means reclaiming the full range of our voice. Not just *how* we speak but *what* we allow ourselves to say. It means no longer apologizing for being passionate, assertive, or unfiltered. It means no longer translating our pain to make others comfortable. It means expressing the truth in our own words, not in the language we were taught to use to be accepted.

Code-switching awareness can be a tool. It can be strategic. But code-switching as performance, when we detach from ourselves to survive, is exhausting. It creates distance from our core. It keeps us in a loop of self-monitoring and second-guessing, wondering if our real voice will be met with judgment or dismissal. Reclaiming our language is about returning to the voice we were given, not the one we were taught to mimic. It's about understanding there is no one way to sound educated, no one way to sound "professional," no one right way to *be*.

Your voice – raw, textured, soulful, unfiltered – is sacred. And we are allowed to speak in a way that honors not just where we are, but where we come from. We don't have to contort ourselves linguistically to be respected. We don't have to speak someone else's version of "correct" to be heard. We get to sound like *us*, fully, unapologetically. The language of suppression may have once been necessary to survive. But now, our truth deserves its own sound. We no longer need to apologize for how it rises.

Rage, Reverence, and the Right to Be Loud

There is a part of me that had to learn my rage was not a problem to fix. It wasn't something to fear, repress, or disguise. It was a message. A truth-teller. A mirror. For so long, Black women's anger has been pathologized, mocked, or dismissed. We've been told to calm down, to lower our voices, to soften our tone. We've been labeled "too much," "too aggressive," or "bitter" before we even finish a sentence. Many of us have internalized that messaging, learning to conceal our anger where it remains unseen, to shield ourselves from being reduced to a stereotype. But our rage is not the enemy. Our rage is sacred. It rises when something is wrong. It flares in the face of injustice. It screams when our boundaries have been crossed too many times. It is not dysfunction; it is data. It is wisdom. It's how the body says, "No more." To be enraged in the face of oppression is not irrational; it is *appropriate.* It is sane. It is necessary.

Rage is not a sign we've lost control. It's often the first moment we *reclaim* it. We must learn to hold space for our anger without shame. To allow it to exist without quickly trying to justify it, shrink it, or make it digestible. There is something deeply healing about saying, "I'm angry," and not needing to apologize for it.

This is about more than release. It's about restoration. When we finally stop gaslighting ourselves, when we stop trying to rationalize the harm done to us, we begin to locate the power in our emotional truth. We learn that rage, when witnessed without judgment, becomes a portal to something deeper. It becomes the energy we use to create boundaries that protects us. It becomes the fire we need to stop tolerating what has never been okay. It becomes the fuel to transform our lives – not through vengeance, but through clarity.

There must be safe places for us to unravel. To wail. To rage out loud. Without explanation. Without performance. Without being told we're "overreacting." The emotional silencing Black women endure, especially around anger, doesn't just suppress our voices; it disrupts our sense of identity. The "angry Black woman" trope is not just offensive. It's harmful. It punishes us for being human. It forces us to choose between expressing pain and being taken seriously. And in that false choice, we learn to betray our emotions just to feel safe.

I learned to give myself grace, and when I did, the buried rage began to show. It came out emotional, tangled, and unfiltered, because I'd never been taught how to give shape to my feelings through calm, verbal expression. That skill wasn't modeled for me. Expression wasn't something I was given the space to practice; it was something I had to figure out on my own. But the more I evolved and embraced myself, the more I chose tenderness over judgment. I stopped blaming myself for not knowing. I started learning how to sit with my anger without letting it consume me, and without shaming myself for feeling it. When I learned to give myself grace, I could finally extend that same grace to other women.

My office became a sanctuary. A place where women, especially Black women, could come to speak freely, to put the weight down. Some days we'd spend hours circling a topic, working through the emotional layers of it until something clicked. One sister might not have the words, but another would step in and say, "I think what she's trying to say is…" We created language together. We co-signed one another's truths. We validated what so many of us had spent years being told was "too much." Those moments weren't just therapeutic, they were transformative. We were learning, together, that rage didn't need to be hidden. It needed to be heard.

We are allowed to be loud. We are allowed to be furious. We are allowed to say, "This is not okay," and mean it with our full chest. Our rage does not make us dangerous; it makes us honest. It tells the truth when no one else will. The aim isn't to suppress our anger; rather, it's to allow it to guide us back to ourselves. It's about recognizing what we've been enduring we no longer need to accept. To let it become the boundary, the clarity, the redirection. Rage, in its rightful place, becomes medicine to be honored, witnessed, and channeled into protection and peace.

We don't owe the world our composure, especially when that composure costs us our voice, our sanity, or our health. There is nothing more powerful than a Black woman no longer afraid of her own anger, who has stopped trying to make it smaller, quieter, or more acceptable. Because when we stop apologizing for being loud, we finally get to hear ourselves again.

Sounding the Sacred: The Healing Voice

Our voices were never meant to be buried. They were meant to rise. To carry truth. To stir memory. To call in something sacred. The healing voice is not just about what we say, it's about what we release, what we reclaim, and what we reawaken. It is sound as medicine. Expression as reclamation and breathe as a bridge. From humming, singing, and chanting to storytelling and truth-telling, Black women have consistently utilized sound to process pain and express their power.

There is wisdom in the way our foremothers used their voices – often subtle, but always intentional. Their humming while tending to daily labor wasn't aimless. It was a rhythm of resistance. A quiet declaration of self in spaces that tried to erase them. Those soft melodies were not just soothing lullabies to children; they were soothing lullabies to the self, reminders of presence, of lineage, of hope. That same hum lives in our chests now, dormant in some, awakened in others, but always available, waiting for us to remember its power.

Singing, too, has always been a sacred act. It has carried us through sorrow too deep for words, joy too expansive for speech. It is one of the few places where we are not asked to justify our emotions; we are simply allowed to feel them. To let them stretch across octaves and into corners of ourselves we often neglect. Whether alone in the car or gathered in communal celebration, that act of vocal release restores something ancient and intimate within us. It is not about performance. It is about presence. And permission.

Chanting, with its repetition and resonance, has long been a tool to bring us back into our bodies, especially when trauma tries to pull us out. A single phrase repeated aloud, again and again, becomes a mantra that moves through the nervous system like a healing balm. It gives the mind something to hold while the body begins to exhale. In that act, the voice becomes an anchor not just to the moment, but to the self beneath the noise.

Somatic voice work reminds us expression begins in the body. The throat is not separate from the heart or the gut; it is their messenger. When we allow ourselves to vocalize without judgment, we begin to hear the body speak in its own language: sighs, groans, exclamations, even silence. All of it is valid. All of it is sacred. There is healing in simply letting sound move. You don't need perfect words. You don't need eloquence. You just need honesty and breath. Because breath is where it begins, it is the quiet foundation of every sound we've ever made. A held breath can stifle not only the voice but the truth beneath it. When we begin to breathe fully, intentionally, we create space for speech that is not performative but embodied. We speak not just from our mouths but from our feet planted on the earth, from the root of our being. And the difference is unmistakable.

To use your voice as a spiritual practice is to enter into a daily ritual of remembrance: I am here. I am whole. I am allowed to take up space. Whether it's in the way we say our own name, the way we pray out loud, or the way we share a story that's lived too long inside, the act of speaking with presence affirms our aliveness. There is a deep joy in that. A joy in singing just because it feels good in your body. A joy in letting your laugh fill a room without shrinking. A joy in using language that feels like *home*, even when it's not considered "proper." A joy in hearing your own voice rise in truth and not pulling it back. These moments are not trivial. They are transformational.

This is the essence of embodied speech: it is not a performance seeking approval, but rather a profound declaration of one's presence. When we speak with breath and clarity, we don't just communicate; we connect. We remember ourselves. We let the voice be an extension of the body's knowing, not a mask to appease others. Reclaiming the healing power of voice means honoring every version of it, the silent voice, the loud one, the trembling one, the one still learning to trust itself. It means understanding the sound of your truth is not a problem to be corrected. It's a rhythm to be restored.

We have learned to intellectualize our experiences, to explain our pain in a way that makes others comfortable. But healing doesn't live in over-explaining. It lives in expressing. In sounding. In daring to make noise in a world that trained us to be quiet. You don't need to be a singer. You don't need to speak "perfectly." You only need to be willing to make space for your own voice. To let it take up room in your body again. To let it guide you back to parts of yourself that words alone cannot reach.

When Black women reconnect with their voices, unfiltered, unashamed, unafraid, we don't just speak. We vibrate. We recalibrate. We resurrect something within us that cannot be colonized, cannot be crushed, cannot be controlled. Let your voice sound like you. Let it carry your story, your sorrow, your joy, your wisdom. Let it tremble. Let it rise. Let it be a witness to your becoming. Let it heal.

Becoming the Author of Your Life

Silence doesn't just affect what we say out loud. It also quietly shapes the stories we tell ourselves in the dark. Over time, it becomes the hand that edits our inner dialogue, refining our dreams into something more acceptable, more tolerable, and more survivable. We start to write ourselves into roles we didn't choose: the strong one who never needs help, the agreeable one who swallows discomfort, the responsible one who always holds it together. After enough time, we forget those roles were written for us, not by us.

This section invites us to remember we are the authors of our lives. Not just the narrators, not just the characters; we hold the pen. With that pen, we are allowed to tell the truth in its fullness. Not just the palatable parts. Not just the polished ones. The messy truths, the changing truths, the sacred truths that don't always fit inside someone else's template. Reclaiming authorship is not about pretending we were never shaped by outside forces. It's about acknowledging those forces and choosing, with clarity and compassion, what still belongs. Narrative liberation begins when we pause to ask: Whose voice have I been carrying? Whose story have I mistaken for my own? What parts of me have I kept in parentheses, waiting for permission to be seen?

To speak into a new reality requires more than courage. It requires tenderness. It means sitting with the old narratives to understand, rather than shame. To honor the younger self who adopted those beliefs out of protection. To thank her for surviving the pages she was given. And then, gently, to offer her a new plotline. One that includes desire. One that allows for joy, for contradiction, for becoming.

This is where intention meets agency. This is where we stop rehearsing inherited scripts and begin to improvise with our truth. Where we stop waiting for someone to tell us what's possible and start narrating our lives with language reflecting who we *are*, not who we've been expected to be. And in that rewriting, the voice becomes something more than just a tool for communication. It becomes a compass, anchor, and legacy. It serves as a means for us to reconnect with our true selves when the world attempts to exclude us from our own narrative. Speaking your truth is not about being loud. It's about being aligned, letting your voice carry your becoming.

There is profound strength in voicing what was once inexpressible. Sharing your growth as it unfolds brings healing. Embracing the idea that you are permitted to revise, evolve, and create something new offers a sense of liberation. You don't need anyone else to validate the chapters you've lived through. You are the only one who knows how far you've come, how many edits you've made along the way just to survive. And now, you get to choose: What do I want to name myself? What story do I want to live into next?

This is not about perfection. It's about presence. It's about honoring your voice, not just as a means of expression, but as the authoring force of your life. You get to tell the story. You get to shape the meaning. You get to take the silence that once muted you and use it as punctuation in a narrative that finally sounds like you. This is how we reclaim power, not through performance, but through authorship. This is how we become whole, not by erasing the past, but by writing the future with intention. And this time, the story belongs to you.

Think about how you've been taught to silence parts of yourself, your needs, your grief, your brilliance. What is the cost of that silence? Consider one truth you've been afraid to say out loud. What might shift if you gave it language, gave it air? You don't have to shout to be heard. Start with a whisper if you must, but let it be yours.

Chapter 13
BECOMING MY OWN STANDARD

An exceptional power arises when a Black woman decides she no longer needs to measure herself by anyone else's yardstick. It doesn't happen all at once. It comes in waves, in the moments when you fill out who you are, when you no longer chase attention to feel seen, when you finally understand your life is not up for consensus. You decide you will not remain confined to boxes crafted for you to inhabit. You are here to live in your full truth, to create, to define, and flourish.

Becoming my own standard meant learning to trust my own rhythm, the way I move through the world, the things that bring me joy, and the values that ground me. It meant choosing alignment over approval and releasing the need to explain my becoming to anyone who wasn't built to understand it. It meant honoring my desires without shame and letting my voice be heard by those who once tried to make me feel invisible.

I spent too long trying to meet expectations never made with me in mind. I became fluent in the language of performance, skilled in the art of shapeshifting, constantly trying to outrun judgment or rejection. And yet, no matter how hard I worked, no matter how polished I became, I still felt like I was chasing a moving target. It was exhausting. It was lonely. It was unsustainable.

So, I chose myself. I chose to pause, to listen, to return to myself. I began to see the most sacred standard I could ever live by was the one I set for myself with compassion, honesty, and grace. I stopped trying to mold myself into someone else's vision of success, beauty, or worthiness. I stopped waiting for someone to affirm what I already knew deep down: I am already enough. As I returned to my true self, I discovered that softness is not a performance, nor a stance, and it is not something I owe the world in exchange for acceptance. My softness is sacred. It is not up for public consumption. It is reserved for those who meet me with care, with respect, with reciprocity. I do not hand it over to spaces that demand my strength but offer no safety. I do not offer it to those who have only ever wanted to extract from me. My tenderness is not weakness; it is discernment. It is the wisdom to know who is worthy of access to the most vulnerable parts of me.

This isn't about perfection or arrival. It's about freedom, the kind that allows you to love your reflection without needing to edit it. That gives you permission to move more slowly, dream differently, and live expansively. It's choosing to live with integrity, even when that makes other people uncomfortable. It's knowing your beauty, your wisdom, your way of being, exactly as it is, is more than enough.

To become your own standard is to stop asking for permission and start embodying your power. It's a reclamation of wholeness. A declaration that you define you. And in doing so, you don't just liberate yourself, you light a path for every woman still trying to remember she was never meant to be a copy of anything.

The Illusion of Arrival

We've been led to think that peace, bliss, and a sense of worthiness are found only after achieving certain milestones. The story goes that once we reach a specific goal, obtain a title, earn a degree, receive a promotion, purchase a home, or enter a relationship, we will finally be complete. We'll rest. We'll allow ourselves to exhale. But that moment rarely comes in the way we expect. The finish line keeps moving. When our value is tethered to a destination, we become perpetual seekers, always chasing, rarely arriving.

For years, I chased the glass ceiling with everything I had in me. And every time I broke through, I thought I'd finally made it. But each breakthrough revealed yet another ceiling above it, thicker, higher, more demanding. What was once a dream milestone quickly became another step on a ladder that seemed to have no end. I told myself I was progressing, but in truth, I was exhausted. Still proving. Still striving. Still silently asking, *"Have I finally earned the right to rest?"*

I had to sit with myself and ask the question I spent most of my life avoiding: *Why do I always feel like I have to be achieving, accomplishing, producing?* Why couldn't I turn my brain off? Why did stillness feel like a threat? The answer came quietly but clearly: I was still trying to define myself. I hadn't yet internalized success in a way that allowed me to claim peace and rest without guilt. I'd met external benchmarks but hadn't given myself internal permission to just *be*.

The finish line culture rewards performance, not presence. It conditions us to equate busyness with value and repose with laziness. I kept going, not because I wasn't successful, but because I hadn't cultivated a definition of success that allowed me to *receive* my own success. I hadn't made room in my life for softness, rest, or the quiet knowing that I was already enough.

Letting go of the illusion of arrival doesn't mean we abandon ambition. It means we stop abandoning ourselves in the name of ambition. It means we stop sacrificing our well-being for applause we may never receive. It means we begin to understand rest is not a reward for productivity and peace is not the aftermath of achievement. Peace embodies presence, signifies alignment, and is cultivated in the present moment.

There is no magical moment when everything clicks and you suddenly feel complete. There is no mountaintop where the doubts vanish and life becomes effortless. Instead, there are small, sacred choices each day, to trust yourself, to value your evolution, to make room for ease without earning it. When we release the lie we must become someone "better" before we are allowed to feel whole, we begin to honor who we are right now. Not in spite of what we haven't accomplished but because we are already worthy.

Self-Definition Without Permission

There comes a point in every woman's life, especially for Black women, when she realizes she can no longer outsource her identity to what she does, how others see her, or what roles she plays. Titles, job descriptions, accolades, even the opinions of those closest to us can start to feel like cages dressed up as compliments. For a long time, I let those external validations define me. I let them tell me who I was allowed to be, how much space I could occupy, and what parts of myself were acceptable to reveal. I didn't even realize I was waiting to be told who I was. I had internalized the belief someone else held the final say, whether it was a boss, a partner, a parent, or a system. I mistook their recognition for truth. I let their approval dictate my worth. I wore the titles they gave me, not knowing that what I truly needed wasn't their validation; it was my own permission. Permission to be fully, freely, unapologetically myself.

For so long, I moved through life trying to earn my existence. I performed. I pleased. I perfected. I confused achievement with acceptance and success with selfhood. I believed that if I could just do enough, be enough, prove enough, then maybe I'd finally feel at home in my own skin. But what I was chasing was never outside of me. It was the voice I had silenced, the part of me that knew who I was long before the world began assigning me roles I never chose. And even as I collected accolades, I felt the dissonance growing inside me. Those titles never truly knew me. They couldn't hold the complexity of my being. They were never built to contain my nuance, my softness, my rage, my ambition, my tenderness, or my brilliance.

The moment I stopped asking for permission to be myself was the moment I realized I'd been handing the pen writing my story to everyone but me. There is something radical, liberating even, about deciding you no longer need to be defined by your job title, your relationship status, your social image, or anyone else's expectation. That you can exist beyond the labels. Your identity is not a fixed destination but a living, breathing truth you get to return to, rewrite, and expand as often as needed. You can begin again, not because you were lost, but because you now know how to honor your growth.

Choosing to define myself on my own terms meant releasing the grip of perfectionism. It meant allowing myself to shift without shame, to desire more without guilt, to let go of what no longer fit, even if others didn't understand. It meant honoring every past version of me that once helped me survive while grieving the ways I had to contort myself to be palatable, acceptable, or safe. And above all, it meant reclaiming the authority I had unknowingly given away.

Now, I speak from a place that doesn't need validation to be real. I choose titles that reflect who I am, not who I'm expected to be. I give myself the freedom to evolve, to change my mind, to shift course, to expand beyond the boxes I was once praised for fitting into. Self-definition is not a single declaration. It is a daily practice. A remembering. A reclamation. It's saying, "I will no longer wait to be seen; I will see myself and stand in that truth." It's choosing to name yourself, not in rebellion, but in reverence. It's realizing you don't have to keep showing up as a version of yourself that was only ever meant to be temporary. For me, that meant untethering from the idea that consistency meant staying insignificant and who I was yesterday had to be who I remain today. That's a lie. We are allowed to evolve. We are allowed to shift. We are allowed to outgrow the identities we once clung to.

We are allowed to begin again, not because we failed but because we've grown. Because we know more now. Because we feel more now. Because we trust ourselves more now. There is power in choosing yourself, again and again, in every new chapter. There is liberation in saying, "I get to change. I get to define. I get to evolve." This is not about perfection or constructing a flawless image. It's about wholeness, making peace with your truth as it unfolds and learning to love who you're becoming, even when others can't recognize her yet.

You are not your résumé. You are not your trauma. You are not anyone's expectation. You are not confined to the stories others project onto you. You are the author of your life. And you never needed permission to become everything you already are.

Making Peace with Your Pace

There is something quietly powerful about deciding your life does not need to be hurried. You aren't late, behind, or failing because your growth doesn't match the speed of someone else. Making peace with my pace wasn't just a lifestyle change, it was an internal shift. It required me to confront the ways I had normalized urgency in my body and spirit. I had come to expect myself to move through life on someone else's schedule, constantly adjusting my speed to meet invisible expectations.

For a long time, I didn't question it. I thought needing to be busy all the time meant I was doing something right. I believed that constant activity equated to productivity, success, and a sense of importance. However, beneath that relentless drive, I felt fatigued. I had become detached from the aspects of myself that craved gentleness. Instead of engaging with life, I was merely reacting to the overwhelming pressure to keep going without pause.

What I hadn't yet learned was that constantly pushing myself to be in motion was less about ambition and more about fear. Fear of being forgotten. Fear of being perceived as not enough. Fear stillness would expose some kind of inadequacy. I didn't realize how deeply I'd internalized the belief that if I slowed down, everything – including my sense of identity – would fall apart.

Making peace with my pace meant finally acknowledging my internal compass had been shaped by systems that rewarded speed over intention. I had to unlearn the habit of assigning value to how much I could accomplish in a day. I had to sit with the discomfort of not knowing what would come next and resist the impulse to fill every moment with doing. It felt unfamiliar at first. I had spent so much of my life focused on what I needed to produce that I forgot to ask myself how I wanted to feel.

Learning to move in alignment with my own timing meant paying attention to the quality of my attention. It meant noticing when

I was stretching myself thin for no real reason, simply because I had become used to the pace. I began to realize the moments when I felt most alive, most honest, were never the ones where I was rushing from one thing to the next. They were the moments when I gave myself permission to be content where I was.

Letting go of the expectation to be constantly available, constantly performing, constantly "on" gave me space to listen. Not just to my intuition but to the parts of me I had ignored. I began to understand pacing isn't just about time; it's also about purpose. It's about choosing how I want to experience my life, not just how I want it to appear.

There is no shame in choosing to move at a speed that protects your peace. There is no loss in honoring what your capacity is, even when the world asks you to give more than you have. You do not need to rush your process and you do not owe anyone an explanation for the pace you choose. Peace came when I stopped trying to outpace myself, stopped measuring my life in units of productivity. I chose to stop treating patience as something that needed justification.

Making peace with my pace is a practice. Not one I've mastered but one I return to again and again. It reminds me I'm not here to be evaluated by how quickly I arrive at my goals, but by how deeply I live in the choices I make along the way. You are not required to match the speed of the world around you. You are not required to be in a hurry to become yourself. You are allowed to feel your way through. You are allowed to move at the pace that allows your truth to rise without being rushed. And when you finally stop asking if you're going fast enough, you begin to ask something far more meaningful: *Is this pace honest? Is it mine?*

Beauty in Your Becoming

Becoming is a remarkable journey. It is not one influenced by external validation or dictated by closeness to another person's ideals; rather, it is the journey you reclaim when you start living authentically from your core. It's a beauty rooted in presence, when you stop looking outward for proof and start honoring what's already within. It lives in your truth, shows up in your decisions, your boundaries, the way you show up for yourself, not because anyone is watching, but because *you* are.

I remember as a young girl watching with wide eyes as my grandmother laid out her satin lingerie at the foot of her bed. She wasn't married, so I didn't understand why she had them or who they were for. One day, I finally asked her, and she said with a soft, matter-of-fact confidence, "Sometimes, you have to get sexy for yourself. Soak in a warm bubble bath, oil up your skin, spray on your favorite perfume, then, with soft satin against your skin, slip into bed and enjoy your own company." Those words remained with me.

She worked three jobs most of the time, always in motion, always carrying more than her share. But what I remember most is not just her strength, it's the way she made space for tenderness. The way she carved out time for herself, not as an indulgence, but as a birthright. Even when the world didn't reward her softness, she kept it alive. She practiced beauty not as performance, but as nourishment. And in that, she taught me something I didn't fully understand until much later: beauty doesn't need an audience. It's sacred when it's just for you.

For so long, I measured beauty by its reception, by how closely I aligned with whatever was praised, accepted, admired. I believed value was something I could earn through appearance, something to be polished and perfected until it pleased others. When I didn't meet those unspoken standards, I questioned my worth. I tried to disappear behind clothes, hair, posture, and silence. But no matter how much I changed on the outside, it never felt like enough on the inside.

Eventually, I had to strip all of that away. I had to unlearn the quiet lies I had been taught that beauty has an expiration date, that it disintegrates with age, that it only belongs to certain bodies. I started to define beauty on my own terms, not by comparing myself to others, but by embracing my own completeness. It wasn't extravagant or attention-seeking; rather, it was understated, grounded, and unwavering. It felt as if I were returning to my true self after years of refinement.

Now, beauty feels like truth. It feels like showing up in my fullness. It feels like choosing clothes that reflect my joy. It feels like a long bath, not because I need to recover, but because I deserve to be taken care of. It feels like adorning myself with intention, not for attention, but for remembrance. I remember who I am when I soften. When I take my time. When I move slowly through the rituals that tell my body, *you are home now*.

There is so much power in creating your own beauty rituals. They don't need to be elaborate or visible to anyone else. They just need to feel like *you*. Maybe it is slipping into something soft and sexy for bed, skin care after a shower, wrapping your hair with care, or lighting a candle and being present with your reflection. These are not vain acts. These are sacred offerings to yourself. They say: *I am worth cherishing, even by myself.*

You are not your size. You are not your age. You are not your image. You are the energy you carry, the voice you honor, the truth you live in. Your beauty isn't up for debate; it is inherent. And you are allowed to redefine it every time you grow. You are allowed to love yourself in the ways the world told you not to. You are allowed to celebrate yourself without waiting for permission. Your beauty is not about being seen; it's about being known. First, by yourself.

Living Beyond the Gaze

There is a difference between being seen and being known. For so long, I thought if I could just be seen, recognized, celebrated, acknowledged, then maybe that would be enough. Maybe the loneliness would quiet. Maybe the doubt would lift. But I came to understand visibility without understanding is its own kind of erasure. People were looking at me, admiring me even, but they weren't really *seeing* me. Not the truth of me. Not the layered, sacred, complex humanity that lived behind my eyes.

As a Black woman, I've known what it feels like to be constantly observed but rarely held with care. To always have eyes on you, evaluating, assessing, judging, while your interior world goes unnoticed. I've been in rooms where my presence was demanded but my voice wasn't welcome. I've been praised for my strength while silently grieving that no one ever asked how I was really doing. That duality is exhausting. Being visible but invisible at the same time, seen only for what I can offer, how I perform, or how well I represent someone else's idea of what a strong, submissive, or faithful woman should be.

There was a time I equated being watched with being valued. I worked tirelessly to stay in good standing with everyone around me. I contorted myself, refining how I dressed, spoke, and moved through the world, all to protect an image. For a while, I thought that meant I was succeeding. But inside, I felt increasingly disconnected from who

I truly was. I wasn't living, I was auditioning. I was pleasing, producing, performing, and losing myself in the process.

Eventually, I had to sit with a question I'd been avoiding for years: *Who am I when no one is watching?* That question unveiled a wealth of insight. It revealed how much of my life had been shaped by trying to be acceptable, respectable, and safe. It revealed how I had permitted the opinions of others—be it in work, relationships, or even within my family—to determine my sense of self-worth. But survival isn't the same as freedom. And freedom only became possible when I chose to stop centering my life around how I appeared and started listening to how I felt.

That shift was subtle at first. It looked like pausing before saying yes to something just because it looked good. It seemed like asking myself, *'Do I really want this, or do I just want to be seen as having it?'* I started making choices that felt aligned with my spirit, not just my image. I stopped leading with strength and started embodying softness, vulnerability, and truth. Yes, it was uncomfortable. It was lonely sometimes. But for the first time, I was meeting *myself* in the process.

Living beyond the gaze means no longer handing your power over to others' perceptions. It means honoring your inner world as the authority, not the audience. It's not about hiding, it's about refusing to shape-shift to fit someone else's lens. It's about choosing yourself with clarity and consistency, even when that choice makes you less palatable, less predictable, less easy to categorize.

The truth is, not everyone will understand who you are when you stop performing. That's okay. Understanding is not a prerequisite for belonging, not the kind of belonging that starts from within. You don't need to be digested by everyone to be valid. You don't need to fit their frame to take up space in your own life.

There is power in living for yourself. In knowing your peace, your presence, and your truth are not up for public debate. In trusting your own rhythm, even when it's misunderstood. You are not here to entertain or prove. You are not here to perform the version of yourself that others are most comfortable with. You are here to be real. To be complete. To be free.

The gaze will come and go. The opinions will shift. But your truth? That's yours. That's your home. And when you begin to live from that place, everything changes, not because others finally see you but because you finally *see* yourself.

The Power of Sacred Standards

There comes a time when you stop asking, *"Is this good enough for them?"* and start asking, *"Is this even aligned with me?"* That moment is often quiet, not dramatic or showy, but it marks a fundamental shift.

It is the moment you begin choosing yourself. Not as rebellion, but as reverence.

For so long, I inherited standards that were never mine. I lived in environments, both personal and professional, where I learned to contort myself in subtle ways. I tolerated discomfort, chaos, and depletion because I thought I had to earn kindness and love. I learned to mistake endurance and silence for maturity. I said yes to things I didn't believe in, stayed in rooms I had outgrown, and poured from an empty cup because I didn't know I was allowed to leave. I didn't know I was allowed to choose differently. But eventually, I got tired – not just physically, but spiritually. I reached a point where I couldn't override my inner knowing any longer. The consequences of abandoning myself became too heavy to carry. And so, I began the work of recalibrating, of returning to my own truth. That is where sacred standards are born.

Sacred standards are not rooted in ego. They're born from clarity, from finally asking, *"What does safety feel like in my body? What does it feel like not to perform, to not pretend?"* They are the internal agreements you make with yourself to stop betraying your peace in exchange for proximity, applause, or survival. They are not about being better than anyone – they're about no longer being less than yourself.

I had to learn how to set boundaries that weren't just about keeping others out but also keeping myself in, within my own integrity, energy, and values. I stopped setting expectations rooted in fear or scarcity and began establishing standards grounded in joy, alignment, and peace. I started believing I didn't have to exhaust myself to be taken seriously. I stopped negotiating my needs as if they were inconveniences. I let go of the guilt telling me it was selfish to prioritize my well-being, and I redefined self-love as choosing not to abandon myself, even when it's uncomfortable.

This is a daily practice, not a destination. It's listening to your body when it tells you you've had enough. It's being honest when something no longer feels good, even if it once did. It's knowing your capacity, your energy, and your joy are sacred, and should not be placed on the altar of someone else's expectations. It's honoring that you are allowed to want more ease. More respect. More alignment. And you do not have to explain why.

My sacred standards taught me I don't owe anyone the watered-down version of myself just to keep the peace. I don't have to stay somewhere that drains me just because I once fought to be there. I can walk away. I can choose again. I can start over, not because I failed, but because I know better now. That's the quiet confidence sacred standards give you: the ability to choose differently with no apology and with deep, grounded grace. And yes, sometimes holding these standards means disappointing people who were never invested in your full well-being. But I'd rather disappoint someone else than continue to disappoint myself.

The life I'm building now is not perfect, but it is mine. It reflects my rhythm, my values, and my desires. It allows me to rest without guilt, to say no without fear, and to speak truth without needing permission. That is sacred. That is success on my own terms.

You are not difficult for seeking to be fully understood. You are not ungrateful for desiring peace, respect, and harmony. You are allowed to want more than survival. You are allowed to want softness, clarity, and truth. And you are allowed to create standards that honor the magnitude of who you are becoming.

This is not about performance, it's about peace. Not about control, but care. Sacred standards are the boundaries you keep, not just with others but with yourself. They are a promise: you will not abandon yourself again. Not for love. Not for validation. Not for anything. And that promise becomes the foundation of a life that is infused with a sense of belonging and purpose, where dreams are nurtured and aspirations take flight.

Ask yourself where you've been measuring your worth.

Who built the yardstick, and did it ever reflect your truth?

What would it mean to build a life around your own

definition of success, beauty, or fulfillment? This is your

invitation to reimagine your standard, not in reaction to the

world, but in devotion to your own wholeness.

Chapter 14
THE NURTURING I NEEDED

A certain type of ache whispers rather than shouts; it simmers quietly. This ache resides in the pauses, the silences, and the spaces where love could have been expressed but wasn't. For many, this feeling has been inherited, passed down through generations, and normalized. It embodies the discomfort of not truly understanding what it means to be held, cherished, or nurtured unconditionally. We were taught to be resilient, to endure, and to excel, yet we often missed out on learning to receive gentle, stable, and secure love.

I recall sitting in a pediatrics course, learning about the distinction between a child's "nurturing" and "naturing" needs and how emotional safety, presence, and affection are just as essential as food or shelter. We touched on neglect and abuse, and how being raised isn't just about being clothed or having a roof over your head but about being made to feel whole, accepted, and deeply loved. Something within me broke apart, as if I had been smacked, and in an instant, memories began to flood in faster than I could catch them.

I calmly rose from my seat and walked out of the classroom, the fresh air hitting my face just as the tears started to fall. My heart ached with a grief I didn't know I had been carrying. I thought of my father, who left when I was five. I didn't find him again until I was twenty-one. And when I did, he told me he had left because he couldn't bear to see my mother love another man. A year later, he was gone again, this time permanently.

I thought about my mother, who went to prison when I was twelve. She wasn't released until I was twenty. I tried to recall hearing "I love you" during those years but the words were faint. Maybe they were never said at all. I couldn't remember being held, couldn't remember the warmth of a hug. So, I made it a point to drench my own children in affection. Physical touch became my love language. I clung to it, offered it freely, because somewhere deep down I knew what it felt like to go without. Outside, I could hardly breathe. Tears came, uninvited but undeniable. My chest ached not from what had just been said but from what had *never* been said.

At a young and tender age, I was never told I mattered just for being myself. No one ever taught me the softness and safety of affection. I learned early how to survive without affection, without comfort, without emotional consistency. I did not know what it meant to be held emotionally, to be wrapped in words and warmth. I was loved but not always *nurtured*. And those are not the same thing.

For a long time, I thought I had escaped the impact. I gave my children what I never had: kisses, cuddles, affirmations, and affection. I held them every chance I got, because physical presence had become my language of love. But that day in class reminded me: I had learned how to be nurturing, but not how to receive it. Not even from myself. That's when I realized I'd become the adult I needed but had never stopped to mother the child still waiting within me.

This is the wound so many Black women carry silently. We are taught strength before we are taught tenderness. We're praised for our resilience, but not for our softness. Many of us grew up in homes where nurture was scarce, if given at all, where love had to be earned, emotions had to be hidden, and survival took precedence over safety. But healing means learning to do what was never modeled. It means creating a kind of care no one taught us but we now choose for ourselves. It's not about romanticizing pain or assigning blame but rather reclaiming the gentle, daily acts of nurture we were denied.

I returned to the little girl I was, the one who sat in silence, who learned not to ask for too much, who mistook self-sufficiency for self-worth. I continue to meet her where she is with grace instead of judgment. I let her cry. I let her rest. I let her be loved, not for what she can produce or fix or hold together, but just because she exists.

Nurturing yourself is not weakness. It is the most radical, revolutionary act of self-love and empowerment. It is how we remind our bones love is not something we have to chase or prove. It is something we *deserve, a*nd maybe, just maybe, we were the nurturers we were always waiting for.

The Ache of Emotional Starvation

The ache of emotional starvation doesn't announce itself loudly. It moves quietly beneath the surface, often misnamed or misunderstood, even by those who carry it. The ache of emotional starvation isn't always born from violence or chaos. Sometimes, it grows in homes that look stable from the outside. Homes where the bills were paid, the meals were made, and the lights were kept on, but where emotional presence was absent. Where no one asked how your heart was doing. Where your tears dried quietly on your own pillow. Where you learned early on not to need too much, not to feel too deeply, not to take up emotional space.

I've come to understand emotional neglect leaves a wound that doesn't always bleed, but it lingers. It forms in the spaces where comfort should have lived, in the unanswered questions, the lack of soothing, the emotional blank stares. It shapes the way we move through the world, not by what was done to us, but by what was missing. That kind of ache is hard to put into words. Hard to hold. Because so many of us were taught to be grateful we weren't hit, or abandoned, or screamed at. But what do you call the grief of never being truly seen?

When your emotional world is not mirrored back to you as a child, when no one names your feelings, validates your experience, or makes space for your complexity, you begin to believe your emotions are burdens. Your sadness is excessive, your joy is too loud, needing reassurance makes you weak. You carry those beliefs into adulthood, still trying to earn the kind of love you never received. Still trying to be "easy" to love, even if it means betraying your needs.

I didn't have language for this for a long time. I just knew something always felt missing, even in the presence of success, connection, or praise. I knew what it was like to perform wholeness while feeling empty. I knew what it felt like to be surrounded by people and still feel emotionally alone. That's the inheritance of emotional starvation: a kind of quiet grief that follows you until you finally name it for what it is.

Healing that ache doesn't happen all at once. It begins with acknowledging your pain is real, even if it wasn't dramatic. That your needs mattered, even if no one ever met them, and you aren't too much for wanting to be understood, nurtured, and held. Slowly, with intention, you learn to give yourself what you were denied. You learn to speak kindly to the parts of you that were never spoken to with tenderness. You learn to sit with your inner child and say, "I see you now."

This ache isn't a weakness. It's a signal. It's your soul asking for nourishment, for presence, for healing. And as painful as it is, it's also an invitation. To no longer abandon yourself. To no longer accept crumbs when you are worthy of care. To stop gaslighting your own emotional reality just because it doesn't come with scars that others can see. Your grief is valid. Your hunger for emotional safety is holy. And your healing is possible.

You are allowed to name what was missing. You are allowed to mourn what you never received. And you are allowed to begin again, with tenderness, with awareness, with love. The ache does not define you – it only points you toward what you still deserve.

When Love Was Conditional

When love is modeled as something to earn, it doesn't feel like love at all; it feels like labor. For so many of us, this was the only form of love we were taught to recognize. It wasn't warm, unshakable, or freely given. It was measured. Tied to acceptance. Conditional upon obedience. It depended on how much we could endure without complaint.

I didn't always know I was living in this state of being. I thought I was just doing what was expected of me. But underneath my striving, caretaking, and ability to push through anything, there was a frightened girl who learned to shape-shift for survival. Somewhere along the way, I absorbed the message my needs were too much, my feelings were inconvenient, and my full self was only welcome in tidy, helpful, high-achieving fragments.

Love, I was taught, was given when I pleased others. When I made things easier for someone else. When I anticipated their needs, suppressed my own, and stayed within the lines. If I stepped out of those lines, if I spoke up, set a boundary, showed sadness, got angry, love would be withdrawn. Affection would become cold. Attention would become distant, and so I learned to perform, not out of vanity, but out of fear. A fear that if I ever stopped proving myself, love would disappear.

This form of conditional love didn't always come with cruelty. Sometimes it came dressed as discipline, religion, or high standards. Sometimes it came from people who were also trying to survive, but the impact was the same. Being strong, capable, and emotionally self-reliant helped me stay safe. Vulnerability was a liability. And what's devastating is how many of us walk into adulthood emotionally undernourished and don't even know it. We function. We succeed. We support others. But there is a quiet emptiness under it all, a longing for love that doesn't ask for anything in return. A hunger to be met in our rawness. To be seen in our full humanity. Not as a provider, a fixer, or a role, but as a person.

Emotional starvation rarely announces itself. It lingers in the background, in our overthinking, our difficulty asking for help, our tendency to apologize for needing anything at all. It shows up in our relationships, where we give more than we receive, in our work, where we burn out trying to prove our worth. In our silence as we swallow pain because speaking feels like a threat to the connection. But here's the truth: emotional illiteracy is not a moral failing. It's inherited. It's passed down in households where survival took priority over tenderness. In communities where children were raised to be strong, not soft. In families where love was withheld to "toughen us up." It's not that we were unloved; we weren't loved in ways honoring our full emotional selves. That absence, that subtle, invisible ache, remains with us.

Naming it was my first step toward healing. I had to admit how much I craved love that didn't come with strings. How much I needed to be affirmed, not for what I do but for who I am when I'm not trying. I had to learn how to give myself what I was never taught to receive:

emotional safety, consistency, patience, and compassion. I had to teach myself I'm not more lovable when I am less messy. My softness doesn't make me weak. Love, real love, holds space for the full spectrum of my being, even the parts still healing.

Unlearning conditional love means honoring your needs even when they're inconvenient. It means letting people in without shrinking yourself and trusting you're worthy of care not because you earned it, but because you are human and here.

The work is tender. It is not always linear. There are days when I still feel the old urge to prove, to please, to earn. But I catch myself now. I remember what I've unlearned. I remember survival is not the same as being emotionally nourished. I deserve love that feels like ease, not labor. We all do.

Relearning What Care Feels Like

There is a quiet disorientation that comes when you start experiencing care that doesn't come with a price. It can feel confusing, even unsettling, when someone offers presence, patience, or warmth without asking you for anything in return. Especially if you weren't raised with those experiences. When care is foreign, receiving it can feel like a language you were never taught.

For a long time, I didn't understand why I flinched emotionally when someone was gentle with me. Why I felt the urge to explain myself, to justify my needs, or to downplay my pain. I'd grown accustomed to spaces where my emotional life was either too much or not even noticed. So, when someone offered affection I hadn't earned through performance or problem-solving, I didn't know how to receive it.

This unfamiliarity didn't mean I didn't want a connection. It meant I had no practice trusting it. It meant I had internalized a way of being where emotional restraint was more familiar than emotional openness. Because no one ever sat me down and showed me what it looked like to be emotionally tended to with care and consistency, I filled in the blanks with silence and withdrawal.

What often goes unrecognized in discussions about love and healing is the weight of emotions we carry, many of which we were never taught to articulate. When you're raised in environments where attention is given to achievement or survival but not to your emotional world, something subtle and long-lasting takes root. You begin to doubt the legitimacy of your feelings. You second-guess the instinct to be comforted. You confuse being overlooked with being independent.

Relearning what care feels like is not a straight path. It doesn't always feel good at first. It often begins with discomfort, with the resistance that comes up when you allow yourself to receive. Whether it's a friend checking in without an agenda or your own decision to sit still and ask yourself how you're doing, care can initially feel too tender to trust. But it's in those small moments, those pauses where you choose to notice yourself, that something begins to shift. It's not about fixing the past. It's about slowly learning what it means to be present to yourself in ways no one ever showed you. It's about acknowledging the unease without judgment and moving toward softness anyway.

Many of us learned to do without affection. We learned to suppress emotions rather than manage them. To push through instead of tending to. That learning shaped us, but it doesn't have to define how we relate now. We can learn to slow down when we're overwhelmed, rather than powering through. We can learn to ask for emotional support without feeling the need to apologize for it. We can learn to see care, not as something earned through hardship, but as something we are inherently worthy of.

This is not easy work. But it is possible. With time, unfamiliar care can become familiar. Not because someone else teaches you how to receive it, but because you begin to believe you're allowed to. Because you start offering it to yourself in ways that feel honest, even if they're not yet easy.

There is no right way to relearn care. It might look like being honest about what hurts. It might look like saying no and meaning it. It might look like giving yourself space to feel before trying to explain.

Whatever it looks like, it begins with the truth: emotional neglect was never your fault and it doesn't have to be your future.

You are allowed to trust care. To learn it in your own time. To experience it without bracing for its disappearance. You're allowed to receive, not because you've earned it, but because you're human, and being cared for is a fundamental human need.

The Inner Mother Awakens

The inner mother doesn't arrive with fanfare. She emerges quietly, often after exhaustion sets in, after another day of holding too much, after realizing that you've been managing, coping, functioning but not truly being cared for. I didn't always have the words for it but I could feel emptiness from tending to everyone else while my own needs went unnamed. There came a point when I had to stop waiting to be nurtured the way I always longed to be and start becoming that presence for myself

Self-mothering isn't about replicating anyone else's version of care. It's not a performance. It's an intimate, often uncomfortable, return to the tender, unsure, or scared places within you and choosing to stay with those parts, even when it would be easier to detach or numb. It's about asking yourself: *What does care feel like for me? What does it look like when no one is watching?*

Learning to mother myself meant recognizing how often I rushed past my emotions, how quick I was to dismiss my needs in the name of being strong or productive. It meant seeing how the way I spoke to myself internally lacked the warmth I instinctively offered others. There was no kindness in the way I pushed through pain or minimized my own longings. I realized I confused self-abandonment for independence. I didn't need another coping strategy. I needed emotional presence.

The inner mother teaches you to stop pretending to heal and feel what's real. She reminds you that you don't need to earn rest, that softness is not a weakness, and that your needs aren't negotiable. She doesn't force you to be okay. She sits with you when you're not. She helps you release the pressure to be constantly composed. And most importantly, she listens – not to fix, but to witness.

Building a relationship with the inner mother takes time. Trust doesn't develop overnight. It comes with time and consistency, grows through constant, quiet gestures, pausing when you want to push through, breathing through anxiety instead of numbing it, and acknowledging the sadness instead of explaining it away. It's checking in with yourself before checking out. It's showing up emotionally in ways no one may have ever done for you before.

There's a distinct grief that comes with realizing you never received certain forms of care when they were most needed. But there's also power in knowing you can begin to give that care to yourself now, perhaps not perfectly, but intentionally. You begin to hold space for your own emotional landscape without judgment. You begin to treat your internal world as sacred.

Mothering yourself means not just building routines but creating a rhythm that supports your actual needs. It's more than taking a bath or writing affirmations; it's tending to your own capacity without guilt. It's knowing when you've had enough and honoring that boundary without needing to explain. It's giving yourself the kind of unconditional regard that allows your nervous system to breathe. It's not just about striving to be healed; it's about being willing to meet yourself with compassion right where you are.

The inner mother doesn't rush your process. She doesn't shame your setbacks. She offers presence, again and again. Through that presence, you learn to trust yourself – not just as someone who survives but someone worthy of tenderness, patience, and peace. You begin to understand safety is not just physical; it's emotional. It's knowing you'll no longer abandon yourself when things feel hard. She is not a fantasy. She is the part of you that shows up when everything else falls away. The more you lean into her, the more complete you feel. You may not have resolved everything, but you've chosen to stay.

Rewriting the Internal Dialogue

For a long time, I didn't even realize the voice inside my head wasn't mine. It had taken on the cadence of people who once held power in my life: authority figures, emotionally unavailable caregivers, a society rewarding my silence and punishing my expression. That internal voice often echoed disappointment and urgency, not love. It told me to retreat before I could be criticized, to perfect before I could be rejected, to fix everything before I even had a chance to feel. I thought it was discipline. I thought it was maturity. Really, it was internalized survival, repeating itself in the quiet corners of my mind.

Many Black women carry this inner dialogue shaped by messages we didn't consent to receive. We grew up in homes where emotional safety wasn't a language spoken. We learned to anticipate others' needs, to earn our place, and to speak softly even when we wanted to yell. When no one teaches you how to tend to your emotional world with gentleness, the voice inside you often becomes a mirror of the world's harshness. We become fluent in criticism, skilled at self-correction, afraid of softness, even within ourselves. Because that voice has been with us for so long, we don't always question its presence. We mistake it for truth. We internalize its rhythm and its tone until we believe harshness is the only path to growth. But that is a lie. One of the most sacred things we can do for ourselves is to question the voice we've inherited and begin to consciously, tenderly, reshape it.

Rewriting the internal dialogue doesn't happen all at once. It's not just about thinking happy thoughts or repeating affirmations when we're hurting. It begins with catching the moment when our default response is to criticize, dismiss, or diminish our own pain. Then, we interrupt that moment with a question: *What would care sound like right now? What would compassion say to me in this exact moment of struggle?* That's how the inner nurturer begins to emerge. Not as a performance or a persona, but as a steady presence, one we build word by word, breath by breath. She is patient. She doesn't rush us to be okay. She doesn't ignore the wound, but she also doesn't shame us for having one. Her voice sounds like warmth. Like consistency. Like, *I see how hard this is. And I'm not going anywhere.*

There's a profound kind of healing that occurs when we finally give ourselves the words we've always needed to hear. Not as a replacement for what was missing but as a restoration of what we've always deserved. With time and intentionality, the harsh voice becomes quieter. The inner dialogue becomes less about monitoring ourselves and more about meeting ourselves. We start to show up for our fear, mess, and longing with curiosity instead of judgment. In those moments, we re-parent something tender and unfinished within us. We create a new emotional foundation, one that doesn't rely on perfection to feel safe, but rather on the radical act of presence. The truth is, we're not unlovable because we were criticized. We're not broken because no one stayed. We are human. And we are still worthy of kindness, especially from ourselves.

When the inner critic rises – and it will – we don't have to push it away. We can listen for what it's afraid of. We can soothe the part of us that learned to be harsh because no one ever showed us another way. And then we can respond differently. Softly. Firmly. Lovingly. Over and over, we get to choose a voice that doesn't abandon us. We begin to trust ourselves through the quiet power of speaking to ourselves like someone we refuse to leave behind instead of silence or self-policing.

Reclaiming the Right to Be Tended To

We were taught to be available. To anticipate needs, to fill in the emotional gaps, to be reliable in moments when no one else could be. In being everything for everyone else, we quietly absorb the belief we aren't allowed to need anything ourselves. Over time, our worth became entangled with usefulness. Our presence with performance. Somewhere along the way, being cared for stopped feeling like a birthright and started feeling like a reward we hadn't quite earned.

This conditioning isn't accidental; it's cultural, generational, and systemic. Black women have carried the weight of being caregivers, often at the expense of being cared for. While it may have kept families afloat, it often came at the cost of our own emotional interiors. We learned to survive without tenderness, to keep going without pause. To give love freely but rarely expect it to be returned in a manner that feels whole or sustaining. Even when we are offered care, something inside of us hesitates, distrusts it, and questions whether we've done enough to deserve it.

Reclaiming the right to be tended to begins with telling the truth about how much that absence has shaped us. It's the truth about what it has felt like to always be the one checking in, the one remembering birthdays, the one showing up, again and again, hoping someone might notice when we're not okay. It's the quiet heartbreak of watching others receive the kind of consistent, thoughtful care we've convinced ourselves we don't need, or worse, convinced ourselves we're too strong to want. But wanting to be cared for does not make us weak; it makes us human. Wanting to be nurtured is not a betrayal of our strength; it's a recognition of our wholeness. The ability to receive, to be softened by someone else's love, to be witnessed in our mess without having to explain or earn it – that is sacred. For many of us, it is foreign. That unfamiliarity is not evidence that we're broken. It's evidence we've been without something essential for too long.

We have to unlearn the silence we were taught to hold around our needs. We must challenge the voice telling us we're safer not asking, we're easier to love when we're self-contained. We owe it to ourselves to push against the reflex that downplays our exhaustion or minimizes our grief so we won't become "too much" for others. These patterns are not signs of personal failure. They are survival strategies that made sense when care was unreliable. But survival is not the same as being nourished. And we deserve more than survival.

We deserve relationships where we're not the only ones reaching. We deserve care without conditions or dependent on how convenient we make ourselves. We deserve rest inside connections holding us without hesitation or resentment. And we deserve to believe being tended to is not indulgent but rather part of how we remember we matter. This reclamation is not about entitlement. It's about balance. It's about creating lives where we are both seen and supported, where we are not punished for having needs, where we don't have to fracture ourselves into pieces just to be chosen. It's about recognizing love is not real if it only flows one way, and it's about finally choosing to surround ourselves with people and environments where our capacity to give is matched by their capacity to hold.

To reclaim the right to be tended to is to deeply believe your well-being is worth prioritizing. Not later, not when you're less busy, not when you've done enough to "deserve" it, but now.

Building a New Legacy of Love

You have the power to interrupt the emotional lineage you inherited. Not because you have all the answers, but because you finally recognize that what was passed down does not have to be passed on.

This section of the journey isn't about rewriting history. It's about creating new patterns from a place of awareness. It's about learning how to nurture in a way born from a grounded sense of self-worth and clarity, not duty, fear, or emotional scarcity.

Many of us were raised in homes where emotional presence was inconsistent. We may have received discipline, direction, even protection, but not always the kind of connection that slows down to listen, affirms without conditions, and sees you fully without requiring performance. That kind of nurturing leaves a lasting impression. Its absence leaves one, too. When we don't have a model for how care can feel, we often recreate what's familiar instead of what's healthy.

This is why unlearning becomes just as important as learning. To build a new legacy of love, we must acknowledge what was missing without shame and then make deliberate choices to create something different. Not louder, not more visible, just more real. We are not here to outperform our mothers or prove we can love better. We are here to be more honest, pay attention to our emotional needs, let presence mean more than productivity, and teach the people we love that being cared for is not a reward, but a right.

We begin to understand love isn't something we earn by staying quiet, agreeable, or selfless. It is something we deserve simply by existing. And when that belief finally roots itself in us, it changes everything. We no longer approach nurturing as an obligation to perform but as an offering that comes from emotional wholeness. We learn to check in with ourselves before saying yes. We learn to pause before pouring from emptiness. We learn to care from a place that does not diminish us.

That's what it means to love from overflow, not depletion. To tend to your own emotional life with the same intentionality you offer others. It's about choosing to rest when you're tired, saying no when something doesn't align, asking for care without guilt, and naming your needs without fear of rejection. It's no longer a matter of waiting for someone to rescue or complete you. It's recognizing you are already whole – that wholeness allows you to love without losing yourself.

This kind of legacy won't always be easy to live out. It may not be instantly understood by family members who were raised to survive, not feel. It may challenge dynamics where your value was tied to your usefulness. But it will feel honest, which in turn creates the kind of safety that can't be faked. When you nurture from this place, your love becomes a steady presence instead of a performance. It becomes something your children, your partners, and your friends can count on, because it comes from a well you've learned to protect.

If you don't have children, this legacy still matters. It's reflected in how you show up in your relationships, your work, and your community. It lives in how you treat yourself in private and respond to your own needs, in how you speak to the parts of you that are still healing. The legacy you're building is not just for others to inherit. It's for you to inhabit. This is how cycles change: not through grand gestures or public declarations but through the daily, deliberate act of choosing a different way to love, starting with yourself.

Think about the care you longed for but didn't always receive. How did you learn to cope with that absence? Have you internalized the idea that needing care is a sign of weakness, or worse, of being unworthy? Now, consider how you can become the nurturer you always needed. What kind of love, presence, or affirmation can you offer yourself today?

JUST LET GO

Letting go is not something that happens all at once. It's a process, a decision you often have to make more than once, sometimes every day, sometimes quietly, with no one watching but you. It is not weakness. It is not abandonment. It is not a failure to hold on longer. It is clarity. It is choosing what aligns with your values, your peace, your well-being, even when that choice is misunderstood. Even when it's hard.

I want you to know reaching this point is not small. It means something that you've made it this far. You've been willing to be honest with yourself. You've dared to look at what you've been carrying and ask, "Do I still need this?" You've questioned what parts of your identity were shaped by pressure, by pain, by performance, and somewhere along the way, you began to believe peace is possible and something you deserve.

This is not about forgetting what shaped you. This is about deciding what you no longer need to carry. So many of us have been taught that release means disconnection, that if we stop holding on, we're letting someone down or giving something up. But what if letting go is an act of deep self-respect? What if it's how you begin again, this time more honest, rooted, and whole? You don't need to shrink to keep the peace. You don't need to explain why something no longer works for you. Letting go can be quiet. It can be slow. It can happen in your own time. You don't owe anyone a performance of closure. You only owe yourself the space to feel what's real and choose what's right.

There is something powerful about naming what no longer serves you and stepping away from it with certainty. You haven't stopped caring; you've started caring for yourself in a deeper way. This is your permission to honor your own limits. To trust that releasing something doesn't mean you've failed. It means you've learned.

Letting go makes room for a new language and new practices, room for stillness, peace, and unconditional joy. Room to breathe without rushing, to live without explaining, to rest without guilt. If no one has said this to you before, let me say it now: you don't have to prove your worth through struggle. You don't have to hold on out of guilt. You don't have to carry the weight of everyone else's expectations. You are allowed to evolve, to say, "This is no longer mine." You are allowed to start again, fully, completely, and without apology. This is your turning point, not because everything is fixed, but because you're no longer abandoning yourself to make others comfortable. You're learning to trust your own wisdom. You're creating space for a life that feels aligned with who you are now, not who you had to be. So let this be your reminder letting go is not a loss, it's an act of love and you are worthy of living from that love, every single day.

Chapter 15

SOFTNESS IS MY SUPERPOWER

"My softness is not a liability. It is a revolution."

We were taught to be strong. To be unbreakable. To push through. To prove. To endure. Those messages were everywhere, spoken and unspoken, pressuring us to remain composed no matter what we were carrying. That kind of strength often became our identity. But over time, the expectation to remain unaffected and always capable started to feel more like a constraint than a compliment. It narrowed our emotional range and quietly distanced us from parts of ourselves we didn't even realize we were neglecting. What the world called strength sometimes came at the cost of our softness, our right to be affected, to be gentle, to need, to feel.

This chapter is about choosing an alternative approach. The strength we learned wasn't wrong but it *was* incomplete. Softness is not the absence of strength; it is the expansion of it. It's the decision to remain connected to ourselves, even when doing so means acknowledging uncertainty, asking for care, or feeling deeply. Softness is rooted in the willingness to stay in relationship with our inner world, even when that feels unfamiliar. It's about no longer bracing against life, and instead allowing ourselves to respond with curiosity and care.

When softness has not been safe or affirmed, learning how to embody it takes time. It takes intention. The shift begins by noticing the instinct to shut down or push through and gently asking ourselves if there's another way. It's choosing to pause instead of performing. It's practicing the kind of emotional presence that doesn't require us to fix everything but to simply witness what's real without judgment. Softness invites us to stop demanding perfection from ourselves and begin building a relationship with the truth of who we are. It is a deep, private decision to show up in a way that prioritizes peace over performance and presence over pressure. It's a refusal to keep living on autopilot, constantly measuring our worth by how much we can handle without breaking. Instead, we begin tending to our needs before they become emergencies. We begin creating space for quiet moments without guilt. We stop justifying rest or gentleness and start honoring them as essential parts of our well-being. That is softness; that is strength.

What once felt unfamiliar becomes the foundation of a new kind of resilience, one that holds us steady through life's unpredictability with grace. Softness allows us to relate to ourselves as a person to care for instead of a project to manage. We begin to trust our emotional experiences, not as weaknesses to correct, but as messages to honor. We discover softness, when chosen deliberately, grounds us. Reclaiming softness reclaims our full humanity. It is not an indulgence. It is not a step backward. It is a return to something we never should have had to abandon in the first place. Softness is the full expression of strength.

Choosing Ease, Gentleness, and Emotional Freedom

Choosing ease, gentleness, and emotional freedom is not always instinctive, especially when you've been taught that survival demands constant vigilance. For so many Black women, myself included, the world outside our homes has never felt neutral. Life is a battle. The moment I stepped outside, I often felt the need to armor up, to be alert, braced for whatever microaggressions, rejection, or dehumanizing encounters might come my way. Racism. Sexism. The subtle ways the world tried to shrink me. I learned to prepare for them, not just mentally but physically, with my shoulders tight, my neck stiff, and my jaw clenched. My body was a mirror of my emotional state: guarded, on edge, and in quiet pain.

I didn't realize how much of my daily experience was shaped by tension until I made the decision to shift. I started practicing intentional relaxation, not just once at night, but throughout the day. Every couple of hours, I would pause and give myself permission to breathe deeply, exhale fully, check in with my body, notice where I was holding tension, and actively release it. In those moments, I visualized the tension leaving me slowly and deliberately, unraveling from the top of my head to the soles of my feet. I made it a ritual, a quiet act of insurrection in a world that never gave me room to rest.

Over time, I noticed a profound shift. I began to live more in my relaxed state than in my guarded one. I smiled more. I slept better. I was more patient with myself and others. The pain that had become my baseline began to ease. I wasn't just surviving anymore; I was feeling myself become more alive. Ease is not laziness. Gentleness is not passivity. They are radical choices. Especially for Black women who have been conditioned to always be on guard, choosing ease means saying, "I deserve rest without guilt. I don't have to carry everything. I can protect my peace as fiercely as I once protected my image." Choosing gentleness says, "I will treat myself with the same compassion I offer others. I will not bully myself into success or healing. I honor my pace and process." Choosing emotional freedom sounds like, "I don't have to suppress my feelings to be accepted. I am allowed to cry, feel, rage, rest, and rejoice. My emotions are sacred data, not problems to fix."

These declarations are not luxuries. They are lifelines. They are a reorientation toward wholeness. When I allowed my body to soften, my heart followed. When I practiced easing my breath, I opened space for a more honest emotional life. And when I learned to soothe myself with intention, I became someone I could trust again. Ask yourself: What does softness feel like in my body? Where do I still resist it? Let those questions guide you, not toward perfection, but toward presence. Toward a life where ease is embodied, not earned. Where gentleness is chosen, not apologized for. Where emotional freedom is a daily practice, not a distant dream.

Redefining Strength Through Softness and Vulnerability

We were often told vulnerability was dangerous and showing emotion made us weak, dramatic, or unstable. So many Black women learned to equate emotional exposure with risk. We were expected to remain composed no matter what we carried inside. We adapted: smiled through pain, laughed through heartbreak, led through burnout, and loved through betrayal. We became fluent in hiding, praised for our ability to endure but rarely asked if we were okay or given room to fall apart without consequences.

Strength that depends on emotional suppression is not genuine resilience; it is merely a form of survival. While survival may have once been necessary, it cannot be the foundation for a life rooted in truth, connection, and joy. True strength is not measured by how quietly we suffer or how well we pretend. It is measured by how deeply we are willing to feel, how courageously we are willing to be seen, and how honestly we are willing to show up, not just for others, but for ourselves.

Vulnerability isn't weakness. It is the refusal to keep performing at the expense of your own well-being. It's saying, "I'm not okay" and letting that be enough. It's asking for help without bracing for judgment. It's trusting you can be seen in your rawness and still be worthy. Vulnerability doesn't mean giving yourself to everyone; it means no longer abandoning yourself just to be accepted.

Letting someone into your truth is terrifying when you've learned exposure can be used against you. That softness can be perceived as a sign of incompetence. That emotion can be misread as instability. We learn to hold it all in, and eventually, the weight of the unspoken begins to harm us more than the fear of being misunderstood. When I discovered my own softness, I began to realize that honesty, vulnerability, and emotional transparency are not weaknesses; they are medicine.

Vulnerability helps us build the kind of relationships that don't require performance. It allows people to see us – not the mask, not the strength we've been praised for, but the truth underneath. It teaches us to receive, to stop over-functioning, and feel worthy of love because we deserve it. Not because we are perfect, but because we are human.

It reflects your journey toward embracing tenderness and an open heart in a world that often encourages us to become hardened. It's about choosing compassion over confrontation and understanding over judgment. As you move gently through life, you find that kindness becomes your ally, and empathy your guide. It takes courage to remain gentle in the face of adversity, to hold onto hope and love when the world challenges you to do otherwise. In this way, you become a beacon of peace and resilience, inspiring those around you to seek harmony and balance in their own lives. This path allows you to connect more deeply with others, fostering relationships built on trust and mutual respect. And that is a radical kind of strength. It doesn't seek to control how we are perceived. It allows us to be seen fully – messy, complicated, evolving – and still believe we are enough.

The more we practice vulnerability, the more we experience unconditional love. The kind of love that doesn't require us to contract, to perform, or to over give. The type of love that recognizes us as whole, even when we're still healing. That is what softness makes room for. And that is the strength I choose now.

Letting Go of Urgency, Hustle, and Hyper-Independence

Urgency is the lie that tells us everything must happen now, or it will never happen. Hustle culture is the lie that says your worth is tied to how busy, productive, or successful you are. Hyper-independence is the lie that says asking for help makes you a burden. Unlearning these lies is one of the most important acts of healing I've ever committed to. Because they weren't just ideas I believed; they were ways I lived. Urgency lived in my breath. Hustle lived in my bones. Hyper-independence lived in my silence. And they all came at the cost of my peace.

Letting go of urgency meant learning to hear the quiet difference between momentum and panic. It meant recognizing how often I rushed decisions, conversations, healing, or growth out of fear that if I didn't move fast, I would fall behind or be forgotten. It required me to tune into a more profound truth: what is mine cannot be missed. Everything meaningful unfolds in alignment, not anxiety. Honoring divine timing doesn't mean inaction; it means trusting that I don't have to chase everything. I can rest, listen, and allow. My life no longer has to be a race.

Letting go of hustle meant confronting the way I once attached my worth to how much I could carry, how much I could do, how exhausted I could become, and still keep pushing. I had to face the quiet discomfort that came with rest, the feelings of guilt, unworthiness, and laziness that had been instilled in me long ago. Choosing rest became a spiritual act. I began to see stillness not as a void, but as a necessary space for restoration, creativity, and joy to return. I had to redefine success, not as endless striving, but as living in alignment with what brings me peace.

Letting go of hyper-independence was maybe the hardest. It meant looking at the parts of me that learned to rely only on myself because I believed I had to. It meant acknowledging the little girl inside me who learned early on needing others was dangerous. That being vulnerable could lead to disappointment, or worse, rejection. But healing required me to soften. To allow help. To let people hold space for me without apology or over-explaining. It meant learning that real safety doesn't come from doing everything alone; it comes from being in relationships where I don't have to.

Softness is not giving up. It's giving yourself permission to stop fighting battles that were never yours to begin with. It's the decision to no longer perform strength in ways that drain you. It's allowing the truth of your humanity to guide your pace, your presence, your relationships. When I stopped chasing urgency, I found clarity. When I stepped back from hustle, I found creativity. When I released hyper-independence, I found connection. In all of it, I reclaimed a sense of freedom I didn't know I had the right to.

Explore your relationship to softness. When did you first learn it wasn't safe? Who taught you that being gentle made you vulnerable in the wrong ways? And now, what does it mean to reclaim softness, not as a performance, but as a power? What does it unlock in your relationships, your boundaries, your self-worth?

Chapter 16
WHEN I FINALLY FELT SAFE

"Safety is not just survival; it is the sacred soil where I finally began to bloom."

For a long time, I didn't realize how much I normalized being uncomfortable. I thought because I could function in an environment, I was safe. I'd adapted so well to environments that undermined me, I stopped questioning whether I should be there at all. I kept showing up, quieting myself, holding in responses, brushing off dismissive comments. I minimized what it meant to be overlooked. I convinced myself that if I was not directly harmed, I had no reason to speak up. But just because something doesn't leave a bruise doesn't mean it didn't hurt. Just because we keep going doesn't mean we're okay.

I learned to tolerate behavior that diminished me because so many of us have been told speaking up will only make things harder. And sometimes, the pressure doesn't just come from those in power but also from people who look like us and have had to adapt too. Other Black women, trying to survive the same systems, sometimes echo the very messages that silence us. They say, "That's just how it is," or "That's the usual," not because they don't care, but because they've been worn down too. There's pain in that kind of resignation, in realizing how many of us have accepted mistreatment as inevitable.

I've been in professional spaces where my expertise was casually dismissed. I've spoken, and my voice was ignored. I've watched conversations move around me as if I wasn't there. Not dramatic, not loud, just consistent disregard. Each time, I told myself to move on, to let it go, to be a team player. But there comes a point when internalizing those moments begins to harden something inside you. You start questioning yourself when, in fact, you should be questioning the culture that makes erasure so easy.

We've been taught to settle for being allowed to be present, as if that is enough. We're told to feel grateful we're even in the room. But real safety is not about being there. It's about being seen and respected while there, being valued without needing to constantly justify our place. It's about being able to express ourselves, ask questions, disagree, and exist without fearing retaliation or dismissal.

Safety is not just physical. It is emotional steadiness. It is knowing your presence won't be used against you. It's the freedom to express your thoughts without filtering every word. It is trusting you won't be punished for telling the truth of your experience. And it's rare, for many of us, especially Black women.

When I finally felt safe, it wasn't because everything around me became perfect. It was because I stopped pretending I was unaffected. I stopped excusing behaviors that hurt. I stopped looking to others to make me feel valid. I began to name what wasn't okay, even if no one else did. I began to trust my own perception. I gave myself permission to stop engaging with spaces that drained me just because I could "handle it." I started prioritizing environments and relationships where I could exhale, where my thoughts and boundaries were respected, where I didn't have to fight to be included.

Feeling safe meant no longer tolerating constant performance. It meant reclaiming my right to feel at ease, to feel stable, to feel whole, not occasionally, but consistently. It meant removing myself from spaces where the cost of staying was self-erasure. It meant acknowledging that what I once called resilience was sometimes just long-term exposure to emotional harm.

Safety, for me, is now non-negotiable. It is my baseline. It is the standard I hold for all parts of my life. And it is no longer something I seek permission to feel.

What It Means to Feel Safe: Emotionally, Spiritually, Physically

True safety is layered. It's not a single moment or a status we arrive at but rather an experience that must exist across every dimension of our being. We're frequently taught to associate safety with basic needs or surface-level indicators: a locked door, a steady paycheck, a roof over our heads. But for many of us, especially as Black women, those markers have never been enough. We've had the job, the degree, the apartment or house, and still felt anxious, unseen, guarded. Because safety is not just external; it's internal. It's the felt sense you are okay *and* allowed to be fully yourself, without penalty, contorting, or asking permission.

Emotional safety is the foundation we don't talk about enough. It's the ability to be in relationships where your feelings aren't seen as problems to fix, where you're not labeled too sensitive or too much for simply being honest. It's knowing you won't be punished, emotionally or socially, for being vulnerable. For having a voice. For crying. For being angry. It's about not having to prepare your words carefully every time you need to express something real. It's the difference between surviving interactions and feeling seen in them. Emotional safety means your truth is allowed to take up space, even if it makes someone uncomfortable. It is the experience of being witnessed and still welcomed.

Spiritual safety is about connection, an authentic, embodied, sacred connection that doesn't require translation or approval. It's the ability to practice your spiritual life without dilution or fear of judgment. For many of us, our spirituality was policed, whether by religion, family, or institutions. We learned to separate our spirit from our truth, to pray in one language while living in another. Spiritual safety invites you back into alignment with what feels *real*. It gives you permission to commune with your ancestors, trust your intuition, and define your relationship with the divine in a way that honors your identity, rather than erasing it. It is being rooted in something greater than you that also flows *through* you, something that knows your history and still calls you whole.

Physical safety is often assumed but rarely honored in the ways that matter. It's more than the absence of violence; it's the presence of peace in your body and surroundings. It's not having to calculate whether you're being watched, followed, or judged for simply existing. It's walking into a space and not immediately bracing yourself. It's not shrinking or tightening because of who's in the room. It's living in a body that's respected unconditionally. Not sexualized, not questioned, not commodified. It's being allowed to breathe, to rest, to move without fear of harm or hyper-awareness. It's not just physical safety from threat; it's the emotional and psychological safety that allows your body to *let go*.

Safety is a full-body experience. It's the unclenching of your jaw, the lowering of your shoulders, the slowing of your breath. It's the absence of fear, yes, but also the presence of gentleness, respect, and care. Safety allows you to stop performing. It allows your nervous system to recalibrate. It gives you space to *feel,* rather than constantly scanning. It invites you to live in your own body as if it were home, not a battlefield. It is knowing you can tell the truth, cry out loud, take up space, and be held – not tolerated, but embraced.

To feel safe is to feel free. Free from the need to prove. Free to stop apologizing. Free to be flawed and still deserving. It means no longer managing others' emotions at the expense of your own. It means making choices from grounded clarity, not conditioned fear. Safety enables us to maintain a healthy relationship with others and ourselves. It lets us dream again. It restores dignity not just in our identities but in our right to exist, whole and unharmed.

Creating Spaces, Relationships, and Habits That Nurture Peace

Peace is not something the world has readily handed to Black women. It is not often waiting for us in the places we've been told it would be, nor is it always found in the systems designed to protect. It is not guaranteed in the spaces we enter, no matter our titles, accolades, or intentions. That's why we must build it. Carefully. Intentionally. Boldly. We don't just stumble into peace. We design our lives around it. We claim it, not as a reward, but as a rightful necessity.

For many of us, creating peace begins with rejecting the deeply internalized belief we should be grateful just to be included. We've been conditioned to stay in places that chip away at our dignity simply because we made it into the room. But now we know better. Peace isn't about being accepted. It's being able to tell the truth and still feel loved. It's being able to feel your own emotions without minimizing them for the sake of someone else's approval.

Creating peace requires reevaluating who gets access to us. It means saying "no" when something violates it, even if we were raised to believe saying "yes" is the polite or expected thing. It means leaving rooms where our intelligence is ignored, our value questioned, or our spirit dismissed. We no longer confuse proximity with belonging. We choose relationships that feel restorative, not extractive. Relationships where we are not just loved for what we give but cherished for who we are.

Peace wrapped in safety looks like protecting your nervous system. It's knowing your triggers, honoring your limits, and building routines that nourish rather than deplete. Sometimes it's lighting candles because the soft flicker reminds your body it's okay to rest. Sometimes it's playing music that quiets the internal noise or covering your walls in art that feels like an offering to your spirit. These are not indulgences. They are reclamations. Safety expands through the relationships we allow to take root. It's not just about how people make us feel in good times; it's about how they respond when we're vulnerable. Do they honor our boundaries without resistance? Do they see us without projecting their own fears onto us? Do they uplift our softness, or do they mistake it for weakness? The people around us matter. Peace requires company that is safe, not just familiar.

We also nurture peace through the habits we choose each day. Breathwork to reconnect with ourselves. Prayer to feel held by something greater. Stillness to hear what our bodies are trying to say. Movement to release what words cannot hold. Journaling to process, not just produce. These practices are not tasks; they are lifelines. In a world that often overwhelms, we need ways to return home to ourselves. Sometimes, creating peace means disconnecting, limiting the news, logging off social media, unfollowing voices that make you question your worth, and disengaging from conversations that do not honor your healing. Not out of avoidance, but out of preservation. Peace is not just about what we let in; it's about what we refuse to endure.

To feel safe is to live without constantly scanning the room for danger. It is to speak and know your words will not be twisted, to rest without guilt, to feel secure in your body, to walk into a space and not wonder if your very presence will be misunderstood, erased, or diminished. Peace is not a privilege for the few. It is a birthright for all. And Black women deserve it, not later, not eventually, but now.

The world may not have been built with our peace and safety in mind but that doesn't mean we cannot build it ourselves, one breath, decision, and boundary at a time. Safety belongs to us because we are here. Our lives are sacred. Our joy is sacred. Our peace is non-negotiable. When we feel truly safe we breathe easier, move differently, and our hearts soften. Our dreams feel reachable. Our love becomes deeper. Our healing becomes achievable, and peace no longer hinges on external validation; it simply exists.

Recall a moment where you felt deeply safe, in your body, in your truth, in the presence of another. What made that moment possible? Think about the conditions that allowed that safety to unfold. What would it mean to seek and protect those conditions now in every space you enter?

Chapter 17
REST AS RESISTANCE, JOY AS JUSTICE

Slowing down can feel like failure. Choosing softness can feel like a risk. And joy? Joy can feel like rebellion.

I didn't always know that. For most of my life, I believed rest was optional, a luxury to be indulged in only after everything and everyone had been tended to. I internalized the lie that if I wasn't exhausted, I wasn't doing enough. That to be strong meant being constantly available. That being a woman of worth meant carrying it all, holding it together, smiling while it hurt, and never asking for help. Especially as a Black woman, I was expected to be tireless, unshakable, unbothered. Even when I was barely holding on.

It's no coincidence. The world has a way of shaping us through pressure, conditioning us to confuse overextension with excellence. The labor we gave freely, the sacrifices made silently, were rarely reciprocated, let alone recognized. Over time, the message became clear: your usefulness is your value. Your output is your identity. You must earn every moment of softness. Every breath must be justified.

So, I moved through life like a machine. I said yes when I was empty. I gave when I was depleted. I poured until there was nothing left but a vague ache I couldn't name. When joy did try to find me, I pushed it aside, convinced it could wait. But it never waited. It faded. So did I.

It wasn't until I sat still, truly still, that I saw the truth. I wasn't living. I was managing. I was performing strength, not embodying wholeness. And I was tired. Not just physically, but spiritually, emotionally worn thin from a life that left no room for me to be soft, to be slow, to simply be. What no one tells us is that the grind hollows you out. Staying in motion for the sake of survival robs you of presence. Being busy all the time is not the same as being alive.

Rest, I've come to understand, is not a passive thing. It is an active, deliberate choice to stop abandoning yourself. It is confronting the discomfort that arises when you stop performing, when you put the to-do list down and realize you've built a life that never included your own needs. Rest is not laziness. It is a radical return to self.

Joy, real joy, is not performative either. It is not found in chasing more. It's found in moments that ask nothing from you but your full presence. A quiet morning. A belly laugh. A long exhale. Not because everything is perfect, but because you no longer require perfection to feel at peace.

This chapter is not about simply slowing down. It's about choosing a different life rhythm altogether. It's about refusing to let exhaustion be your legacy. It's about breaking free from the narratives telling you your worth was conditional, that you had to be palatable, productive, or pleasing to deserve your own care.

When I lie in bed longer than necessary, it is not laziness; it feels like liberation. When I say no to one more obligation, it is not selfishness; it is self-honoring. When I pause, savor, protect my time, tend to my body, and laugh without explanation, I am not just reclaiming moments; I am reclaiming a life that belongs to me.

For Black women especially, this matters deeply. Our rest was stolen. Our joy was policed. Our needs were dismissed. Our softness was misunderstood. We were never meant to survive under that weight, and yet we did. But surviving is not all we were meant to do.

I rest – not because I have nothing to do but because I refuse to keep abandoning myself in the name of getting things done. I rest because my body deserves repair. My spirit deserves ease. My mind deserves quiet. I don't need to justify that. I just need to honor it. When I let joy in, when I allow myself to feel light, to play, to celebrate something without a reason, it reminds me I'm still here. I'm still human. I'm still whole.

This chapter is about that reclamation, choosing your aliveness over your achievements. It is about saying: *I matter. Not after I've produced. Not after I've endured. Now. Just as I am.* Rest is how we return to ourselves. Joy is how we stay there. This is not about indulgence; it's about interruption. About naming that our rest is sacred. That our joy is not up for negotiation. And that we do not have to suffer our way into being seen as worthy.

When I rest, I interrupt the cycle. When I choose joy, I reclaim what was denied. When I slow down, I remember who I am. I do it not because the world told me to but because I finally realized I could.

The Myth of Meritocracy: When Worth Is Measured in Exhaustion

We were told (and shown) we had to work twice as hard to be seen as equal, so we did. We overperformed, we overgave, held the weight of generations in our bodies, and still showed up, still smiled, still succeeded. We thought if we were excellent enough, kind enough, humble enough, educated enough, someone would see us, would finally say, "You belong here."

I spent years holding on to that belief. I poured myself into degrees, certifications, long hours, and leadership roles. I gave from a place so deep I didn't even realize I was emptying myself to be chosen. Beneath the striving was a longing, an ache, to belong. A deep, innate desire to be valued, not just for what I could do, but for who I was. I stayed in spaces where I wasn't seen, where I wasn't celebrated, because I was taught belonging was something you earned and if you didn't feel safe, maybe you just hadn't worked hard enough yet.

Something in me began to shift. Slowly, then all at once. I started to realize the very spaces I fought to stay in were not designed with people like me in mind, not for Black people, not for women. I noticed how often I was dismissed, minimized, and misused. My brilliance was treated like a threat, my presence like a problem to be managed. It hit me: remaining present in a space that does not value you is not belonging; it's betrayal, the slow erosion of self under the illusion of success.

That realization changed everything. It gave me the courage to ask a question I never considered before: *Is this space even worthy of me?* Not just *do I belong here?* But *do they deserve me?* These questions became a turning point. I'd worked hard to become the woman I am: educated, nurturing, loving, and grounded. I began to understand my value was not up for negotiation. My worth wasn't something to be bartered in exchange for acceptance.

The myth of meritocracy tells us if we try hard enough, we'll be recognized. But for Black women, the game has never been fair. We are asked to carry institutions on our backs and then be questioned about our qualifications. We are praised for our resilience, then punished for our boundaries. We're expected to keep showing up, even when we are invisible in the very systems we sustain.

There is a grief that comes with waking up to this, realizing our dedication was never going to be enough, not because we lacked anything but because the system was never designed for us. It's not just a professional grief; it's personal. It's the ache of realizing how long you've spent contorting yourself into spaces that society deemed you unworthy of. There is also power in this awakening.

Once you stop chasing value in people or places that cannot see you, you become free to see yourself. You start redefining success by how much you protect your peace instead of how much you produce. How deeply you choose yourself instead of by who chooses you. You learn to rest without guilt and say no without over-explaining. You walk away without folding yourself into a version someone else can tolerate. Your boundaries are not up for debate. Your worth is not something others get to decide.

Letting go of this myth is an act of liberation. A reclamation of the truth you never had to prove anything to deserve love, rest, or belonging. You were always worthy. You are still worthy. And now, you know it for yourself.

Undoing the Inner Drill Sergeant

Even in the stillness, when the house is quiet, the inbox is closed, and the day is done, the voice doesn't always quiet with it; it lingers. A low hum, familiar and persistent; *"You should've done more today,"* or *"There's still work to do."* It speaks of expectations, in pressure, in shame disguised as motivation. For years, I mistook that voice for discipline, drive, some necessary companion to success. The truth is, it was fear. It was internalized fear trying to protect me from a world that taught me my value depended on how much I could endure without complaint.

That voice was born in systems never designed for me to rest. It is the sound of generational survival, of growing up in a culture demanding Black women be extraordinary just to be visible. That told us to be twice as good to be considered half as worthy. That measured our dignity in output, our belonging in sacrifice. It's the voice shaped by every job where we had to overperform to be taken seriously, every room where we felt like a visitor, every relationship where love had to be earned.

I internalized the grind. I let exhaustion be my metric. I clung to achievement like it would save me from invisibility. I kept moving, kept giving, kept proving, until I realized I wasn't living. I was going through the motions and smothering under the weight of what I thought I had to be to matter.

Undoing that voice, that drill sergeant in my mind, didn't happen through willpower. It happened through compassion. It started by being willing to hear it differently. Instead of silencing it with more striving, I began asking questions I was never taught to ask: *Who first made me believe that productivity equals value? Who taught me that my rest must be justified? Who convinced me that tranquility is idleness, and tenderness is weakness?*

When I embraced honesty, I uncovered a profound truth: that voice wasn't truly mine. It was inherited, shaped by conditioning and rehearsed over time—a survival script passed down through systems and generations. Although it no longer benefited me, its predictability had become almost comforting. However, familiarity does not equate to freedom, and I needed to discover how to rebuild myself without the relentless inner critic.

I started talking to that voice. Not with anger, but with gentleness. I told it: *You don't have to push so hard anymore. You don't have to run on overdrive to be accepted. You are safe now.* The more I softened that inner voice, the more I heard something underneath it, my actual truth. My truth says: *I am not behind if I rest. I am not inadequate if I slow down. I am not selfish for tending to my own needs.*

This is the unlearning. The re-parenting. The sacred reclamation of self. It's not easy. There are still days that voice rises up louder than I'd like, when I feel guilt for a nap or shame for not answering every message. But now I pause. I breathe. I remind myself: *I am not a machine. I am a person. A human being, not a machine, simply in action, and I don't have to hustle to prove that I matter.*

Undoing the inner drill sergeant is not about becoming passive. It's about becoming whole, reclaiming the parts of me that knew rest was essential long before I was taught to abandon it. It's about choosing softness in a world that taught me to be steel. Choosing truth over performance. Choosing joy over perfection. Choosing to belong to myself first. This voice inside me is learning, and so am I. We are both learning how to live without urgency. How to love without condition. How to rest without guilt.

Joy as a Sacred Disruption

Joy, when rooted in truth, doesn't require performance. It doesn't need to be shown or shared or justified. It just needs to be *felt*. That means giving yourself permission to honor what makes you feel complete, even when nobody else understands it. It means no longer deferring joy to the end of a to-do list. It means allowing yourself to be moved by beauty, not because everything is perfect, but because *you're still here*, and that is something.

For me, joy now lives in the mundane. It lives in a warm shower where I let the water hold the weight I've been carrying. It lives in a spontaneous text to someone I love, in dancing barefoot in my kitchen, in the way I allow myself to breathe deeply with no agenda. It lives in the soft moments just for me. I no longer wait for the perfect moment to be joyful. I *create* the moment; I *become* it.

We must admit the truth: the systems surrounding us were never designed to nurture our joy. They benefit when we are too tired to feel, when we confuse being busy with being worthy. When we believe joy is a distraction rather than a form of resistance. However, the truth is, our joy does something policies and platforms never could: it reminds us of our humanity. It affirms we aren't machines. We aren't utilities. We aren't here to serve until we disappear.

There is grief in joy, too. Grief for all the times I didn't know I could feel this light. Grief for the generations before me who weren't allowed to slow down long enough to feel the sun on their face. Grief for the girl I used to be, who mistook over-functioning for success and silence for safety. Joy, this sacred, quiet, uncompromising joy, is also for *her*. For every version of me who thought peace had to be earned, for every part of me that was taught love and rest were luxuries instead of essentials.

Joy is not weakness. It is not naïveté. It is a survival strategy that doesn't rely on depletion. It's a deep knowing *I am worthy of feeling good*. Not just when everything around me is calm, but *especially* when the world expects me to be hardened and disconnected. It's knowing I can access joy in a society designed to make me forget myself. I can return to myself, over and over, through pleasure, softness, delight, and laughter.

When I feel joy, I am no longer on defense. I'm not bracing for the next blow. I'm not strategizing how to protect my worth. I'm resting in it. I'm allowing it to exist without explanation. And that is where the healing lives.

This joy is not optional. It is sacred. It is political. It is personal. It is the way I remain intact. It is the way I teach others how to see me, not through my pain, but through my *presence*. It is the way I honor myself, without needing anything else to change. Maybe that's the revolution: choosing to feel good, on purpose, for no other reason than because I deserve to.

The Quiet Rebellion of Doing Nothing

There is something profoundly powerful about choosing to do nothing as a deliberate, sacred act of self-love. I didn't always know how to be still. I used to fill every moment with noise. Something to do, something to fix, someone to respond to. If my calendar wasn't full, I felt like I wasn't living up to the version of myself I'd worked so hard to become. Somewhere along the way, I began to believe my worth was directly tied to how much I could give, achieve, and accomplish in a day. Beneath all the busyness, there lingered a subtle longing. A part of me pondered how life might unfold if I allowed myself the freedom to simply *be*, without needing to apologize, explain, or perform. When I finally allowed myself that space, I felt something I hadn't felt in a long time: peace. Not the kind that comes after everything is accomplished. But the kind that lives in you when nothing is required.

That's when everything shifted. My deepest insights came not during the hustle, but in relaxtion. The most aligned ideas I've ever had arrived not in the chaos of multitasking, but in the quiet moments when I was lying in bed with the sun on my face or sipping tea without distraction. It was in those moments I started to hear the voice of my spirit more clearly, the voice that knew the way before I asked the question.

I remember one afternoon, sitting in silence, with no music or TV, just the soft hum of the day. I had no plans. I wasn't writing, fixing, or organizing. I was just breathing. In that breath came clarity, a full picture of the next step in my purpose unfolded like a quiet knowing. Not because I forced it, but because I finally made room for it to arrive. I realized: this wasn't nothing. This was everything. That's the lie so many of us were sold: that doing nothing is wasteful, that rest is earned only after exhaustion, that being idle means being less than. But the truth is, reclaiming your time, your stillness, your right to *not do* – that is liberation.

Doing nothing is how I remember myself. How I recover what the world tries to take: my center. It's the breath between the grind and the grief. The sacred pause that brings me back to my own rhythm. It's not an escape; it's a return. There is medicine in slow mornings. In quiet afternoons without productivity. In naps that are not rushed. In staring at the sky without needing it to mean something. There is a kind of clarity that only emerges when you're no longer performing for approval. When you finally understand, your worth isn't in your output.

When I stopped measuring my value by how much I could endure, I started to realize how much I'd been missing. My own tenderness, my own joy, my own voice. I stopped asking, "What should I be doing?" and started asking, "What does my spirit need?" Sometimes it needs sleep. Sometimes it needs silence. Sometimes it just needs time without urgency. And that is valid. That is holy. Quiet is not empty. It is full of truth. It is where we birth our most aligned selves. It's where we hear our intuition clearly, before the world interrupts. It's where our dreams find their way back to us.

This is what I want you to know: you are not lazy for resting. You are not less ambitious for needing quiet. You are not broken because you need to pause. You are allowed to do nothing, and still be whole, worthy, and radiant. So, give yourself permission to slow down. To unplug. To be with your thoughts and your breath and your own beautiful presence. Not because you've "earned" it but because it's yours. Every act of rest is a quiet revolution. Every moment of stillness is a doorway back to yourself. And every breath you take without urgency is a step toward the life you deserve: a life not built on exhaustion, but on ease, clarity, and peace. Doing nothing is not the absence of life. It is the space where your real life begins.

Rituals of Ease and Spacious Living

I had to confront the truth: I didn't know how to just *be*. Stillness felt foreign. Slowness felt dangerous. Ease felt selfish. When I paused long enough to listen, I heard something deeper; my soul was tired of running. I didn't want another checklist, another benchmark, another "grind" to survive. I wanted space. I wanted breath. I wanted *me*.

Rituals of ease helped me find my way back. These rituals are not extravagant or performative. They are quiet, intentional moments that remind me I am allowed to exist without having to earn it. It's waking up and staying in bed for an extra twenty minutes because I deserve to ease into the day on my own terms. It's playing music that makes me feel whole again because my spirit responds to sound.

I began designing my life around rhythms, not routines – fluid, intuitive practices that follow my internal seasons. Some days, that means canceling a meeting just to sit in the sun. On other days, it means cooking a slow meal from scratch, not to impress, but because I enjoy the way it tastes. I no longer see these things as indulgent. I see them as medicine.

Saying no has become one of my most sacred rituals. I no longer stretch myself thin to avoid disappointing others. I do not explain away my boundaries. I don't let guilt convince me to betray my needs. Saying no without apology is how I honor my nervous system. It's how I tell myself the truth: I am not here to be constantly available. I am not here to be drained. I am not here to abandon myself to be understood.

Ease lives in the small moments that say, *I choose me.* It's in the long bath where I relax without rushing. It's in the slow walks where I let my thoughts settle like dust. It's in the tea I sip in silence, where the warmth reminds me I deserve gentleness. These aren't just habits; they're acts of spiritual nourishment. They remind me I am not here to be efficient. I am here to be *well.*

I've noticed when I make room for ease, I hear myself more clearly. The noise quiets. The pressure reduces. In that space, I remember who I am beyond the roles and expectations. Ease is what allows me to create from a place of fullness. It's in those quiet, unhurried moments where my best ideas are born. When I give myself space, I become a vessel for clarity. So many of my most meaningful visions, my boldest ideas, my clearest decisions: they all arrived in rest, not overactivity.

Ease is not the absence of effort. It is the presence of intention. It's a rhythm of living that values your breath over your productivity. In a world that teaches us our worth is in what we do, this is essential. So no, I'm not interested in proving myself through depletion. I'm not waiting until I'm on the brink of burnout to choose myself. I am building a life that infuses peace into my bones. A life where I don't need permission to rest. A life where softness is not postponed until everything is finished, because everything will never be finished.

Rituals of ease are how I come home to myself again and again. I protect them fiercely, not because I'm fragile but because I finally know what I need. I no longer confuse urgency with importance. I no longer reduce my life into a to-do list. I no longer let my body be used for validation.

This is how I live now, in rhythm with myself, with tenderness, intention, and space. If no one has told you, let me say it plainly: you are allowed to slow down. You are allowed to protect your peace. You are allowed to build a life that nourishes you. Ease is not something you wait for. It's something you create, and *you* are worthy of that creation every single day.

Reflect on how often you allow yourself to rest – not just sleep but exist in a state of true ease. Has rest ever felt like a risk? Have you been conditioned to equate rest with laziness, or joy with guilt? Think about how rest and joy are part of your birthright. How can you reclaim them not as rewards, but as necessities?

Chapter 18

SEEN. LOVED. FREE

"When I stopped hiding, the love I had been praying for found me."

We were not taught to trust we could be seen without being judged or loved without conditions. So many of us spent years adapting, curating ourselves to be digestible, productive, agreeable, never too loud, never too angry, never too soft. We learned how to disappear in plain sight because disappearing felt safer than being seen and rejected. But you cannot feel fully loved if you're constantly hiding. You cannot be deeply free if you're still performing acceptance.

There is sorrow in realizing how much of your life has been shaped by the need to be palatable. And there is a power in deciding you no longer want to live that way. When you let your real self step forward, at first it may feel like exposure. But eventually, it begins to feel like freedom. You realize you are not hard to love, you were just too busy bracing for impact to let any love in.

To be seen is not about being watched. It's about being *known*. Fully. Without disguise. Without reduction. Without needing to be useful, pleasant, or perfect. To be loved while being seen is not just intimacy; it is a form of emotional alchemy, where vulnerability and acceptance intertwine to create a profound connection. When someone witnesses your truth, your tenderness, your contradictions, and your quiet stillness and still chooses to love you, a rare bond is formed. It is a sanctuary of trust, a space where authenticity reigns, and where love is not just felt but deeply known. When those two things come together, being seen and chosen, love no longer feels like a distant concept. It becomes embodied. It lives in your breath, your choices, your presence. You begin to trust you can exist without needing to defend your existence. Your story doesn't need to be validated to be real. You learn love is not found in disguising, resisting, or self-betrayal. Sometimes it is found in allowing yourself to rest in your own truth, without apology.

Healing your heart space is an intimate journey that doesn't require public acknowledgment or validation. It's a deeply personal, internal experience. By embracing self-love, you allow yourself the grace to explore your emotions and discover your true self. This journey demands patience and compassion as you gently navigate through both past wounds and cherished joys.

Love signifies the beginning of a profound return to your authentic self. This true self isn't shaped by external expectations, past traumas, or survival instincts; it reflects the essence of who you have always been, hidden beneath societal pressures. It allows your heart to embrace love from others without the weight of rejection, discomfort, or fear. Key elements of this transformative experience include establishing a strong foundation of confidence and acceptance, which empowers the creation of meaningful connections. It involves recognizing that being seen is a sacred experience and understanding that being loved while visible is revolutionary. Experiencing true safety when you are both understood and treasured is central to this process.

This journey marks the moment when you no longer seek permission to occupy space, cease negotiating your vulnerability, and stop fighting for your worthiness. When a Black woman experiences this kind of liberation—without armor and without apology—she transcends mere healing; she becomes a beacon of resilience and empowerment. She moves through the world with an unwavering sense of purpose, her spirit unburdened by societal constraints. Her story becomes a tapestry of not just courage but grace, woven with threads of her ancestors' wisdom and her own hard-won truths.

Putting Down the Armor and Allowing Love In

For so long, emotional strength was our survival tactic. We learned early how to hold our feelings tightly, how to keep our feminine tenderness under lock and key. Emotional tenderness was seen as a disadvantage, even dangerous. We were told it made us too vulnerable, too exposed, too dependent. So, we tucked that tenderness away and became skilled at managing our image. Holding it together. Showing up ready. Always composed. Always prepared.

We wore our strength like a second skin. Not just to protect ourselves from the world, but to shield us from the fear that if we allowed even one moment of vulnerability, everything might fall apart. In doing so, we built up a wall, not just around our hearts but around our entire emotional being. We became masters at giving love, pouring into others, anticipating needs, and reading rooms. But when it came time to receive, we froze. Not because we didn't want it, but because we didn't trust it. We weren't sure what it would feel like to be seen in our rawness and still be loved.

So many of us wear masks to feel safe. Masks of competence. Of perfection. Of emotional invincibility. But over time, those masks become heavy. The deeper we bury our need for connection, the more disconnected we become from others, from our truth, from our own hearts. We start to feel invisible in relationships that should feel intimate. Misunderstood in rooms we've spent years proving ourselves in. Tired of showing up for people who never truly see us. We wonder why we feel untouched, unloved, and unknown. But love cannot touch what we keep behind the mask. Love cannot reach the places we've hidden in shame or silence.

Letting down the armor is not about becoming defenseless. It's about becoming honest. It means acknowledging where we're still afraid to be soft, where we're still performing well, and we're still seeking validation through effort rather than allowing ourselves to simply be. It means asking ourselves: What am I still protecting? Who taught me I had to earn love? What would it feel like to be loved without the mask?

The truth is, we don't have to be exceptional to be loved. We don't have to be perfect to be worthy. We don't have to break down to deserve being held. We are allowed to receive love without having to prove ourselves first, to be met in our wholeness rather than our pain, productivity, or sacrifice. Our *wholeness*.

Letting love in doesn't start with others getting it right. It begins with giving ourselves permission to believe we are lovable now, as we are. It means turning toward the parts of ourselves longing for affection, reassurance, and intimacy, and no longer shaming them. These parts are not needy. They are not weak. They are human. When we allow those parts to come forward, we begin to live from a place of more profound truth.

To let down the armor is to create space inside your own life where you can exhale. "I no longer have to operate from a place of fear. I can choose to lead with love." It serves as a gentle reminder: "I deserve to be loved, even as I navigate the journey of learning to love myself." Furthermore, it's a serene yet potent affirmation: "I believe that the person I am underneath the facade is deserving of recognition and connection."

This is not about recklessly opening yourself to everyone. It's about discerning where you've been hiding from yourself. It's about saying, "I don't need to harden to protect my heart," and "I don't need to withhold softness; I am softness." It's about creating emotional safety inside your body first, so that when love does show up, you don't push it away out of fear or hesitation.

Removing your armor is not a sign of weakness. Rather, it is a profound return to the essence of love. When you allow yourself to be seen completely, truthfully, and tenderly, love not only seeks you out; it acknowledges you. When that happens? You don't have to chase it. You simply allow it to come closer. To meet you. To hold you. To love you, not because you've suffered enough to deserve it, but because you deserve it.

The Joy of Being Fully Seen Without Apology

To be seen without apology means knowing your feelings, thoughts, and ways of existing do not need to be corrected. It means being listened to when you speak and not having your words rephrased to sound more acceptable. It means being able to show emotion without being questioned, having your needs respected without being made to feel excessive.

It is the experience of being around people who pay attention to how you move through the world instead of just to what you say. They don't need you to explain yourself to respect your boundaries, your decisions, or your values. They're present enough to witness you as you are, not as an idea, not as a label, not as a version of you they prefer, but as the real person standing in front of them.

This joy does not come from being celebrated. It comes from not being dismissed. It comes from finally recognizing you no longer need to justify your existence or over-explain your choices. It stems from understanding there's nothing wrong with how you show up when you're protecting your own well-being rather than someone else's comfort.

To be fully seen means you no longer wait for permission to be yourself. You no longer reduce your reality to keep things smooth. You no longer monitor your emotional responses for acceptability.

You give yourself the space to be honest in real time. This is where the joy lives: the space of honesty without tension, without guilt.

This is not about needing approval. It's about no longer fearing rejection. It's about reaching a place within where you don't expect to be misunderstood the moment you express a feeling or state a need. Where you don't assume telling your truth will cost you a connection. Clarity doesn't come from changing the world; it comes from changing what you expect for yourself.

The most profound joy of all is when you look in the mirror and realize your recognition matters most. You see yourself with complete clarity and accept what you see, not as a project to fix or a role to perform but as a whole person, worthy of being heard, worthy of being chosen, and most importantly, worthy of being known.

Radical Self-Love as Resistance and Revolution

In a world that profits from your insecurity, where systems were built on the belief your body, voice, emotions, and power must be controlled or softened to be accepted, choosing to love yourself is not a casual act. It is a stance. A disruption. A refusal to carry shame that was never yours. In a society that has repeatedly forced Black women to choose between being heard and being liked, being soft and being taken seriously, being assertive and being called angry, radical self-love challenges every one of those false choices. It says: *I am not here to be palatable. I am here to be whole.*

Radical self-love begins the moment you stop trying to prove your worth. You stop tying your value to your job title, relationship status, body shape, or emotional resilience. You stop looking to external validation to confirm what your spirit has always known: you are enough. You don't need to do more, prove more, give more, or explain more just to exist without punishment or erasure.

It's choosing to stop apologizing for your needs. It's being honest about your limits, even when others don't understand them. It's sitting with your own discomfort instead of abandoning yourself to ease someone else's. It's turning down opportunities that come with the cost of your peace. Radical self-love is not performative self-care; it's rooted in discipline, boundaries, and clarity. It requires you to unlearn what you were taught to normalize, to stop tolerating what harms you just because it's familiar.

It's no longer hiding your brilliance for the comfort of others. No longer waiting to be seen by those who only notice you when they need something. It's no longer aligning yourself with people or systems that expect you to retract, transform, or compromise who you are to be accepted. You begin to rest, not because you completed everything, but because your body deserves to recover. You let yourself be tranquil, not because you earned it, but because you no longer accept exhaustion as a badge of honor. You stop chasing proximity to power and remember your power was never lost, it was simply buried under the weight of silence, expectations, and the need for survival.

Radical self-love is about choosing yourself before others try to claim, name, or use you. It's looking in the mirror and not needing permission to feel good about what you see. It's being deeply connected to your inner wisdom because you trust yourself more than the noise outside of you.

This love is generational work. It's how we shift the blueprint we hand down. It's how we teach our daughters their softness doesn't make them weak, their brilliance doesn't need to be hidden behind humility. Their bodies are not sites of shame, labor, or debate. It's how we model for our sons that love does not require domination, and power does not need to come at the expense of someone else's freedom.

Radical self-love is political because it refuses to comply with systems profiting from our pain. It dismantles the myth we must constantly endure to be worthy. It asserts you don't have to be broken to deserve care. You don't have to shrink to deserve belonging or be exhausted to deserve rest. When a Black woman begins to live from that place, she accepts herself in full, not waiting for the world to catch up or for systems to grant her dignity, she becomes rooted. Not louder.

Not harder. Just rooted. Clear. Certain. And from that place, she chooses her life instead of constantly defending her right to it.

When You Are Seen, Loved, and Free.

When I started to genuinely embrace life, I recognized that I had spent countless years merely existing, functioning, showing up, and completing necessary tasks without truly being present. I wasn't grounded in joy or anchored in authenticity. My journey appeared resilient on the surface yet felt empty within. I was unaware of this reality, believing that merely surviving was sufficient and that acting well was equivalent to feeling complete. However, the instant I felt truly seen—deeply seen—I started to understand the difference.

Living is not about how well I can check the boxes or navigate systems. It's about waking up and feeling like I'm allowed to be here exactly as I am. It's laughing from a place untouched by fear. It's crying and not feeling the need to apologize. It's giving myself permission to speak, rest, and create without running it through someone else's expectations first. Living means I don't monitor myself in real-time. I don't calculate how I'll be perceived. I just show up.

I used to love with a wall still up. I didn't know I was doing it. I thought I was just being careful, protecting myself. But the truth is, I was afraid – afraid that if someone saw all of me, especially the parts that didn't look polished or impressive, they'd leave. I've had people love the version of me I curated to make them comfortable. I know what it's like to be admired but not known. I know what it's like to let that continue just to feel close to someone. When I began to love without fear, when I stopped hiding the parts of me that felt too sensitive, too needy, too complicated, I started to feel the world shift. Not because people changed, but because I did. I no longer saw love as something I had to earn by bending. I started trusting I could be met without shrinking, and I was. I am. Love touches differently when it's not filtered through survival.

The more I opened, the more I aligned. I didn't have to chase, persuade, or tolerate anymore. I began to feel the quiet power of choosing. I chose myself. I chose peace. I chose relationships where I could breathe. I released what made me question my value. Not in a dramatic, performative way. But in the still, clear knowing that *this no longer serves me*. That was the beginning of freedom.

Letting go wasn't easy. It never is. But it created space. And in that space, I felt something I had never truly felt before: ease. Not just rest. Not just relief. The ability to be in my body, in my life, in my joy, without performance. I didn't have to explain it. I didn't have to justify it. I could just *be*.

Now, I don't live to impress. I don't love from fear. I don't speak from survival. I live in the fullness of who I am. I love with both feet planted. I speak with softness and certainty. I don't brace myself every time someone gets close. I'm not waiting to be hurt. I'm not holding back pieces of myself to stay safe. This is what it feels like to be seen, loved, and free: I'm no longer trying to be the version of myself that makes everyone else comfortable. I feel completely at ease and at home within myself.

Think about what it means to be fully seen. Who has loved you without needing you to be smaller, quieter, or more convenient? Where are you still waiting to be seen like that? Now ask: How can you start seeing and loving yourself that way first, fully, unapologetically, and without delay?

Chapter 19
FINALLY LETTING GO

"I do not have to carry it all. I do not have to be it all. I am enough, just as I am."

For a long time, I was unaware that I could truly live by those words. I understood how to achieve success, endure challenges, and consistently show up to give my all, even when I felt completely drained. However, the ability to simply *be*—without the need to perform, strive, or prove myself—was a lesson I had to relearn, or perhaps, uncover for the first time.

Letting go was not an overnight transformation; it began with a gentle whisper. A subtle truth emerged on a day when I felt weary, not just in body but in spirit. I was exhausted from the endless pursuit of feeling adequate, weary of stepping into spaces that only recognized my utility and overlooked my humanity. I was tired of justifying my worth to those who had no desire to appreciate it. Yet, amid that fatigue, a different kind of strength began to surface—not the kind I was taught to wield for survival, but one that encouraged me to soften, to surrender, and to prioritize myself.

This moment was not an ending, but the dawn of a new chapter in my life. The beginning of a life that no longer requires me to contort myself to fit roles that diminish me. A life where I am no longer required to carry the emotional weight of others. A life that invites ease as a natural rhythm. I am learning, sometimes gently, sometimes through tears, that letting go is not the same as giving up. It's an act of courage. It's an act of reclaiming what was always mine: my time, my joy, my breath, my becoming.

Living in my softness as power means embracing a strength that is not a weakened version, but rather a complete redefinition of what strength truly is. A softness that sets boundaries without guilt. That rests without needing justification. That chooses peace over struggle. A softness that allows me to feel it all, grief, rage, pleasure, delight, and know that I can hold all of it without being consumed.

The beginning I'm stepping into now does not ask me to minimize myself to fit someone else's idea of who I should be. It doesn't require me to be everything for everyone. It doesn't demand constant sacrifice just to be seen. It honors the truth I'm already whole. I always was. All the degrees, accolades, and sacrifices never made me worthy, they only distracted me from remembering that I already was.

In this new beginning, I receive love without question, because I know I am worthy of love. I receive joy not as a fleeting moment, but as a resting place. I receive rest not as a break from labor, but as a natural part of life. I no longer wait for permission to feel good. I no longer wait for the world to make space for me. I am the space. And that is more than enough.

Living this way means I've stopped living by the rules that said I had to be silent to be safe, be invulnerable to be respected, and earn love by overextending myself. That story has ended. And in its place, I am writing a new one. One where healing is the standard, not the exception. Where my softness is not a liability, but a sacred inheritance. Where my safety, my dignity, and my joy are not things I have to chase, but things I claim, right now, exactly as I am.

This new way of being is still unfolding. There are days I feel the pull of the old ways – the need to prove, to perform, to please. But now, I pause. I breathe. I remember I am already enough. I don't need to do more to matter. I don't need to earn what I was born deserving. I don't have to be the strongest woman in every room. I just have to be me.

Letting go has brought me back to myself. To a self that is not exhausted, not hardened, not hidden, but whole, free, alive. I am not returning to the old story. I am moving forward with my own. This time, I'm moving gently. I'm moving truthfully. I'm moving freely.

A Vision for a Life Where Black Women Are Free to Just Be

Imagine a world where Black women don't have to explain themselves before they speak, where we are not praised only when we perform but also when we persevere through unthinkable pain. A world where our value is not measured in sacrifice, our brilliance is not questioned, and our softness is not seen as a threat. A world where being is enough. That is the world I crave. That is the world I am learning to believe is possible.

In this world, we are not defined by our resilience; we are honored for our *existence*. For our breath. For the simple truth we are here, alive, and deserving of every good thing. It is a world where we don't have to be ten steps ahead just to be seen as competent or have to trade parts of ourselves to feel safe, palatable, or accepted. In this world, we are allowed to show up messy and whole, unfinished and worthy. We are allowed to be complex. We are allowed to be *human*.

The transformative power of healing is immense, with the potential to be both generational and revolutionary. Imagine the profound impact it would have, as if we were finally returning to our true selves. When Black women heal, they create a ripple effect that transforms everything around them. They redefine how they love, parent, lead, and connect. The shift moves from giving out of depletion to giving from a place of abundance. There's a cessation of apologizing for their needs, replaced by a newfound trust in their right to receive. A healed Black woman is not merely a gift to herself; she becomes a reflection for every other Black woman striving to remember who she was before the world dictated who she should become.

In this world, rest is not something we steal in the cracks of our schedules; it is built into the foundation. We don't question our right to feel light. We *expect* it, we *claim* it, we *protect* it. We are no longer the emotional laborers of everyone else's comfort. We are no longer asked to break ourselves to make others whole. Instead, we design our own spaces, sacred, slow, and nourishing. Places where our nervous systems can permanently regulate, where our hearts can expand, where our truths can land without being dismissed or distorted. In these spaces, our tears are welcome. Our rage is understood. Our brilliance is never doubted.

In this world, we love ourselves. Deeply. Daily. Without conditions. We do not wait for others to tell us we are enough. We know it. We embody it. We live it. Our dreams aren't filtered through fear or approval-seeking; they are pursued with fire and clarity. We stop trying to prove and start allowing ourselves to become. We trust we are worthy of softness, of celebration, of peace.

This vision is not merely a fantasy; it is already coming to life each time we release what was never ours to bear. Every moment we cease to measure our worth by the struggles we've endured, and every choice we make to prioritize presence over performance. It begins when we question the systems that have convinced us we must earn our rest, when we unlearn the falsehood that we must be everything to everyone to be loved, and when we look into the mirror and recognize someone who is not broken but rather whole.

This represents a return—a reclamation—a quiet uprising that starts from within. It involves letting go of the narrative that our worth is tied to suffering, relinquishing the silence we once used to survive, and shedding the armor we wore for protection, and allowing ourselves to finally feel free. We deserve to be embraced, to heal, and to live lives that resonate deeply within our being, not just lives that appear impressive on paper. This is not only attainable; it is ours to choose.

In this choice, this radical, sacred, unapologetic choice to be, we begin to build something truer. A world, and a self, where Black women can finally *just be*.

An Invitation: Just Let Go

It may seem straightforward, even gentle, but in reality, it is a bold and courageous invitation. It's not a one-time event, a single moment where everything falls into place and the weight disappears. No, this is a continuous practice. A daily reckoning. A sacred and essential journey back to your true self, time and time again.

It sounds so gentle. So easy. But for many of us, especially Black women, it is anything but. This isn't just a poetic idea. This is soul work. Generational work. It is the quiet revolution of loosening your grip on the roles you were taught to perform. The masks you had to wear. The expectations that buried you under their weight. Letting go asks something real of you. It asks you to face the parts of yourself you've been avoiding. The pieces of your story that you tried to rewrite through overworking, over giving, and overachieving. It prompts you to examine the beliefs you've inherited about what makes you lovable, safe, and valuable, to reflect, and to ask: *do these beliefs still serve me, or are they slowly suffocating me?*

Letting go is a sacred practice, a return, a remembering. It means showing up and choosing yourself each day, even when your voice shakes. Even when everything you've learned says you shouldn't. When you've been conditioned to carry it all, to hold the burdens of everyone else, perform excellence without pause, it takes radical courage to set even one thing down. It is terrifying. It means facing who you are without resistance. It means asking, *what if I stop performing strength? What if I stop earning my right to rest? What if I stop trying to prove my worth?* For so long, I believed my value lived in my ability to hold it all together without breaking. In the ease with which I smiled through pain. I've learned, slowly and painfully, survival is not the same as freedom. Holding it all together is not the same as being whole.

This invitation is not light. It's not shallow. It demands something deep. It requires the courage to confront the fears and insecurities that have quietly shaped your decisions: being misunderstood if you speak your truth, being too much, not being enough. The fear of being alone when you stop performing the version of yourself others have grown used to. Letting go means saying, *I no longer want to carry what was never my burden to hold.* It takes deep, wide compassion to forgive yourself for the times you stayed too long in places that hurt you, to offer grace for the seasons when shrinking was your only way to survive. To honor the versions of you that did the best they could with what they had. Letting go isn't about disowning those selves; it's about thanking them and then releasing the need to keep living in their patterns.

We don't let go from a place of weakness. We let go for clarity and peace. It is an act of deliverance. A fierce declaration: *I will not be defined by trauma. I will not be reduced to survival. I will not perform wholeness; I will embody it.* It is the moment you realize you don't owe your worth to a job, a relationship, a degree, or a performance. You don't need to contort yourself to be loved. You already are. Letting go is a declaration you are no longer waiting to be chosen or waiting to be freed. You are the one choosing now. You are choosing to trust your softness is not a liability, your rest is not a privilege, and your voice is not a disruption. You are choosing to nurture the parts of yourself you once silenced, the parts that crave peace, that long to be seen, that desire rest without guilt.

Letting go is disruptive. It shakes what is familiar while bringing you home to what is true. It says: *I am not here to be palatable. I am not here to be perfect. I am here to be whole.* It means reclaiming the fullness of your humanity. Reclaiming your joy. Your breath. Your stillness. It's no longer waiting until everything is healed to live. It's choosing to live now, messy, miraculous, whole.

This invitation is not just for a better life. It's for a truer one. You don't have to ration your joy. Your worth is not a negotiation. Your rest is not delayed until you earn it. It's a life where you get to exist in your softness. Your beauty, your brilliance. Without apology. This is your beginning, one rooted in presence rather than performance. In peace, not protection. You are no longer bound by the old rules. You don't have to hide to be safe. You don't have to prove to be seen. You don't have to hustle to be whole. This invitation is open. It's yours. Not just today but tomorrow and the day after that, and every day you choose yourself again.

When Holding on Hurts More Than Letting Go

There's a deep ache that comes from holding on too long to people, roles, or identities that once served us but now sit heavy on our spirit. We don't always notice the pain right away, especially when we've been taught clinging is noble, loyalty means staying, and strength is proven by our endurance, so we grip tighter. We tell ourselves discomfort is just part of growth, that maybe if we just hold on a little longer, try a little harder, suppress our needs a little deeper, things will shift. But eventually, the cost becomes undeniable.

The things we once clung to for protection slowly begin to erode the parts of us we were meant to preserve. The relationships we hoped would nourish us start to fracture our self-trust. The beliefs we inherited about being good, strong, dependable, begin to feel like cages. And the perfectionism we once wore like armor begins to crush the very softness we long to feel.

This is the moment many of us find ourselves unsure of whether the pain of holding on is still safer than the unknown of letting go. What if letting go isn't failure? What if it's reorientation? A refusal to keep bleeding for stories that no longer reflect your truth? We must stop mistaking self-betrayal for strength. Stop confusing emotional overextension with loyalty. These ideas, these quiet, persistent myths, have been passed down and enforced through generations. For Black women in particular, they are often embedded as survival code: carry it all or lose it all. So, we hold on even when it hurts. The truth is, pain is not proof of purpose.

Letting go is not about walking away from love or responsibility or care, it's about redefining what love means when it costs you your sense of self. It's about choosing integrity with yourself over the performance of strength. It's about knowing when something once essential has become too heavy to hold without fracturing your spirit.

Letting go doesn't always happen with grand gestures. At times, it may appear as though you are being uncooperative or withdrawn. Not responding to the text that always leaves you anxious. Saying "I'm not available" without guilt. Letting your voice tremble as you speak a boundary. Releasing the role of fixer, savior, or the one who always has it together. It looks like naming what's no longer aligned, even if no one else agrees. Even if no one else claps. When you've been defined by what you've endured, release can feel like failure. But it's not. It's maturity. It's self-respect. It's you reclaiming your right to exist on your own terms.

Letting go is not forgetting who you've been. It's honoring who you no longer need to be. It's also not abandoning everything you've learned. It's discerning what you no longer need to carry. This is about alignment, not detachment. Choosing peace doesn't mean you never loved what came before. It means you're willing to love yourself enough to stop hurting for it.

We must release the myth our suffering is what makes us worthy. That martyrdom earns us belonging. That being the one who "never gives up" makes us admirable. Sometimes, what's most courageous is not holding on but rather choosing to let go with tenderness, reverence, a deep bow to who we were, and a soft welcome to who we're becoming.

You do not have to fracture yourself to prove your devotion. You are allowed to outgrow people, places, patterns, and beliefs. You are allowed to heal, even if it means disrupting the story others expected you to stay in.

Letting go is not a loss; it is a choice. It is the decision to no longer compromise your peace for the sake of appearances. It is clarity. It is sovereignty. It is saying: I choose to live in alignment with who I am, not who I had to be to survive. You are not leaving anything behind that was meant for you to become.

Softness Is a Strategy

Softness is not passivity; it's power without force, grace without submission, and strength in gentleness. It is the subtle art of resilience, where one can bend without breaking and stand firm without aggression. It's the quiet courage to evolve without explanation. It's how we choose peace in a world that profits off our pain, and it's how we protect what's sacred within us.

We were never meant to survive by hardening, but life, especially for Black women, has demanded it. We have been conditioned by culture, history, and systems that were never designed for our freedom, that strength means being rigid, unyielding, and impenetrable. That anything resembling softness is a liability, so we became what we thought we had to be: indestructible. We put on a covering made of excellence, endurance, and self-sacrifice. This may have kept us moving but it also kept us disconnected from our own tenderness.

Softness is not just a luxury, indulgence, or afterthought. It is a strategy for survival and liberation. It means honoring your nervous system enough to stop running on empty. It means telling the truth about your limits, your needs, your longing for more ease. It's a decision to tend to your body with care, rather than pushing it past the point of breaking. It is saying: I no longer accept burnout as a badge of honor.

Softness is intelligence rooted in self-trust. It knows rest is not a reward; it is a requirement. Silence is not always peace; sometimes softness speaks in clear, unwavering boundaries. Vulnerability is not fragility; it's freedom. For Black women, softness can feel risky.

We've been conditioned to equate visibility with danger, vulnerability with exposure, and emotion with instability. But the truth is, we don't owe the world anything. We don't owe anyone the hardened version of ourselves. We don't have to be impenetrable to be safe; we only need to be grounded in ourselves.

Softness invites us to stop bracing for harm and start building lives that feel gentle to live in. It means allowing yourself to feel without judgment, to cry without apology, and to be tender with your wounds, knowing that healing doesn't always look fierce. It often looks like stillness. It looks like asking for help. It looks like grace. That's not weakness – that's strategy. The world will always benefit from your over-functioning if you let it but you deserve to benefit from your own being.

Softness reconnects us to our humanity. It slows us down long enough to remember what we've ignored: our bodies, our breath, our spirit's call for quiet. It teaches us to honor ourselves without condition, simply because we exist. Because we are here and enough. When we allow it, softness becomes a space of safety within. A place where you no longer need to brace, to overperform, to overexplain. A place where you can let your shoulders fall, unclench your jaw, and breathe without fear of being seen as less. Where you can ask yourself, not what do I need to achieve, but what do I need to feel safe, to feel nourished, to feel whole?

This is the shift. This is the transformation. Softness liberates us from the myth we were born only to carry. It refuses to define us by how much we can endure. Instead, it invites us to live. To feel joy without guilt. To access pleasure without delay. To claim peace without justification. It is a strategy because it's sustainable. It doesn't require you to burn out to be valid. It builds a life that feels like yours. It gives you permission to stop surviving and start becoming the person aligned with your own truth.

You do not have to suffer to be worthy or push to the edge to be seen. You get to choose softness deliberately and unapologetically as a way of reclaiming your breath, your body, and your being. Softness is wisdom. It is the kind of power that doesn't shout but speaks volumes. Embracing your worth is about the serene acknowledgment that you are sufficient, especially when you find yourself in a tranquil state. If you have been searching for validation, here it is: Permit softness to guide your approach, let tenderness embody your truth, and welcome rest as your means of revolution. Because you deserve a life that feels good to wake up to. Not after you've proven yourself. Not after you've healed everything. But now. Today. As you are.

Letting Go as a Spiritual Practice

Letting go is not about detachment; it's about deep, sacred trust. Trust that what is yours will remain. Trust that rest is not retreat, it is reverence. Letting go, in its truest form, is not a passive act; it is a spiritual alignment. A conscious, embodied returning to the truth you were never meant to carry everything alone. It's the quiet revolution that begins when you decide control is no longer your compass and urgency is not your home.

This kind of surrender is not about giving up. It's about giving yourself over to your intuition, your ancestors' wisdom, the natural rhythm of your becoming. It's choosing to listen to the sacred language of your body when it whispers, "It's safe to exhale now." It's allowing your spirit to rest without explanation, your heart to soften without apology.

Letting go is a spiritual act because it requires you to trust in what you cannot always see. It asks you to believe in the unseen forces carrying you this whole time, your ancestors who dreamed of your healing, your inner voice that still speaks beneath the noise, your breath that keeps returning to you no matter how many times you forget. This is not the kind of trust that's hurried or naive. It is ancient. It is practiced. It is felt in the marrow.

You are not surrendering to a system that has asked you to disappear. You are surrendering to your knowing. You are surrendering to timing that isn't rushed by capitalism or coerced by fear, to the understanding ease is not a betrayal of your strength; it is a holy return. And you're beginning to see that what you thought was strength, the overextension, self-neglect, perfectionism, was often survival masquerading as control. But now, survival is no longer your only option. Now, you are being called to thrive.

This spiritual practice of letting go is an act of reverence for your own life. It's how you declare: I no longer need to grip so tightly to pain, to stories that diminish me, to roles that no longer fit. It is a sacred reclamation of your space, your peace, your presence. It's completely acceptable to take your time as you navigate this journey; it reveals itself day by day. On some days, you may find it simple to let go, while on others, you might face challenges. This is all part of the experience. What truly counts is your commitment to keep coming back.

Embracing the power of letting go signifies trusting that your healing journey doesn't need to be dramatic to be profound. Stillness can be sacred, as the divine connects with you not through perfection, but through your presence. Your body possesses wisdom that transcends words, and your emotions are not burdens but valuable aspects of your experience. Furthermore, your moments of rest are not signs of laziness; they are acts of worship.

This is ancestral work. You are doing what many before you never had the space or safety to do: lay burdens down. Break cycles. Choose softness. Choose truth. Choose liberation. You are not just releasing the weight. You are reclaiming the space it took up. The space where your joy lives and your clarity begins to flourish. As you navigate this path, you are honoring those who came before you, weaving their hopes and dreams into the fabric of your own journey. Embrace this opportunity to create new traditions rooted in love and understanding. As you continue to choose liberation, know that you are paving the way for future generations to walk their own paths with courage and grace. Your journey is a beacon of hope, a reminder that change is possible and that the future is bright.

Letting go is a prayer in motion. It is how we honor the sacredness of being alive without needing to earn it. It is how we, unapologetically, reclaim our authentic selves. You are not failing when you choose peace or weak for wanting ease. You are in a state of remembrance, and with each release, you are transforming into the person you have always intended to be: liberated, complete, guided, loved, and profoundly supported by the divine.

Letting Go Doesn't Mean You Don't Care

We were taught love means holding on no matter what. But love is not bondage. Love, at its best, frees everyone involved. Letting go doesn't mean you've stopped caring. It doesn't make you cold. It doesn't make you selfish. It means you've chosen to care for yourself in a world that never taught you how. It means you're learning love without boundaries becomes obligation, and devotion without self-respect becomes self-erasure. Letting go is a declaration your well-being is no longer a negotiable matter.

Too many of us were conditioned to confuse love with misery. We were handed a version of loyalty that required us to disappear inside of it. It taught us to bear what broke us in the name of connection. As we outgrow those roles, patterns, and people, we are made to feel guilty, as if choosing ourselves was a betrayal.

Releasing is not the same as rejecting; instead, it embodies the highest form of honesty. It conveys that I can genuinely care while still acknowledging when something no longer aligns with me. I can love you and still say this dynamic is no longer healthy for me. I can remember the good and still move forward, because the cost of staying has become too great. Letting go is not the absence of love; it is the arrival of clarity.

Sometimes, holding on hurts the most because it no longer fits who you are. Letting go is not a dismissal of your past; it's an acknowledgment you've grown beyond it. This growth is sacred. It means your healing is working. It means your boundaries are sharpening. It means your self-worth is no longer tied to how long you can endure.

Letting go doesn't erase the story. It honors the chapters while acknowledging the book must move forward. You're allowed to change your mind. You're allowed to evolve. You're allowed to say, "This is no longer enough for the woman I'm becoming." That's not cruelty. That's consciousness. Still, the grief is real because even necessary endings are painful. Even aligned release requires mourning. You may still ache for what once felt like safety, even if it came at the cost of your spirit. You may still miss the idea of someone more than the reality of them. And that's okay. Grief is not a sign you made the wrong choice; it's a sign you loved, you invested, and you showed up fully. That matters.

There comes a time when loving yourself means releasing the beliefs and relationships that ask you to betray yourself to stay connected. A time when peace matters more than perception. When authenticity becomes more urgent than approval. And when your own aliveness – not how much you sacrifice for another's comfort – becomes the measure of love.

Letting go is a return to sanity. It's saying, *I don't have to hold it all to prove it mattered. I don't have to stay to validate my love. I don't have to embrace pain to be seen as committed. I get to love from a place that honors my peace, not erases it.* Letting go doesn't mean you don't care. It means you care differently now. It means you've learned the deepest kind of love does not demand your silence, your suffering, or your smallness. It invites your wholeness. That is the kind of love you're learning to offer, starting with you.

Softness as the Doorway to Companionship

For so long, I believed I had to be hard to be safe, that my guard was the only thing standing between me and betrayal, that my sharp edges would keep the pain out, even if they kept love out too. Maybe that was true back then. Perhaps the walls were necessary in a world that had not yet learned how to care for the heart of a Black woman. But now, I'm learning something new. Something softer. Embracing softness not only defines how I present myself, but it also paves the way for genuine companionship.

It makes space for honest, nourishing connections. It allows you to show up without pretending and to be close to others without abandoning yourself. For Black women, softness has often felt risky. We've been taught to be pillars, not people. To give endlessly, hold steadily, and endure quietly. Tenderness has rarely been celebrated in us; instead, we are often celebrated for our tenacity. That tenacity, while sacred, can sometimes turn into isolation. It can leave you surrounded, yet unseen. Softness interrupts that pattern. It says, "I don't have to brace for harm to feel strong." It reclaims the right to be gentle, to be cared for, to be real. Not hardened by the world but rooted in truth.

Softness is not about smiling through discomfort or being more palatable to make others stay. It's the radical act of showing up exactly as you are, without apology, without defense. It's how we unlearn the myth love must be earned through suffering. It's how we remember companionship is not built on sacrifice but on mutual recognition and safety. Softness clears space for that kind of clarity. When you move beyond survival mode, your vision sharpens: you can identify those who honor your boundaries, those who truly listen to you, and those who completely embrace you. You start to understand that closeness without emotional safety isn't intimacy; instead, it leads to exhaustion. You stop pursuing mere proximity and begin to prioritize genuine connection.

This kind of connection, this form of love, does not require losing your sense of self. It doesn't require your silence or shapeshifting. It asks for your truth, your quiet, your joy, your rage, your rest. It meets you where you are, not where you're performing from. It honors your softness not as a liability, but as a sacred boundary, one that says: only those who are gentle with my humanity can stay. This scared boundary says: I will no longer confuse love with labor. I will no longer trade pieces of myself for the illusion of belonging. I will no longer explain my tenderness away to make others feel more comfortable. My softness is not an invitation for harm; it is a signal of my self-trust.

Companionship, the kind that heals instead of harms, cannot grow in the soil of self-neglect. It doesn't survive where your needs are dismissed, or your voice is buried. It blooms where softness lives, where you can rest without fear, where you are heard without raising your volume, where you can be quiet and still be held. This shift in how we relate doesn't mean everyone will come with us. Some people only knew us through our armor. Some were never equipped to meet our softness with the care it deserves. But those grounded in their own healing will not be threatened by our gentleness. They will not require us to harden to be loved. They will see our softness as a language they've always longed to speak.

Let this be your threshold: You don't have to betray your tenderness to survive a connection. Softness is the doorway, not only to companionship with others but to deep, lasting companionship with yourself. From that sacred place of inner union, the right relationships will recognize you. Not because you contorted yourself to be loved, but because you chose to stay soft enough to be found.

This is the Beginning

Letting go is not the end. It is not a finish line, a closed door, or a quiet goodbye. It is the turning of the page. The first breath after the release. The moment when you stop surviving and start *living*. This is the beginning, not just of a new chapter, but of a new language, a new rhythm, a new way of being.

You have devoted years, perhaps even decades, striving for acceptance in environments that left you feeling unfulfilled and restrained. You have become adept at emotional suppression, engaging in continuous giving that keeps you valuable yet invisible. And now, here you are, standing at the edge of a new life. A life no longer asking you to betray yourself to belong. This is what begins when you let go: you cease seeking permission to embrace who you genuinely are. You stop apologizing for your tenderness, scars, and emotions. You stop defending your worth. You cease to engage in discussions where your insights are disregarded or your wisdom goes unnoticed. You stop pretending that being the one who keeps everything together defines your entire identity.

This new beginning is not loud. It doesn't come with grand declarations or dramatic shifts. It arrives quietly, in how you move differently, how you speak to yourself, how you choose peace without needing to justify it. You begin to trust yourself because you remember who you are. You honor your boundaries without guilt. You receive love without suspicion. You choose yourself instead of waiting to be chosen.

Embracing softness as your strategy transforms your guiding principles. While the world remains unchanged, you have evolved. You've chosen to recognize that you don't owe anyone perpetual sacrifice. You now understand that your softness is a form of wisdom, reflecting your truth and representing your divine right to live freely.

In this new beginning, love is celebrated rather than constrained; joy is embraced in the present rather than deferred. Rest is not a reward to be earned; it is honored and valued. You shift from living for the future to fully embracing your present. You attract alignment because you no longer feel compelled to present a version of yourself that's disconnected from your soul.

This journey isn't about transforming into someone entirely different; it's about becoming *more* of who you've always been. It involves unlearning the beliefs that led you to feel you needed to harden, hustle, or hide in the first place. Stop negotiating your worth. Stop compromising your peace. Stop asking for less, so others feel more comfortable. This new chapter is yours to embrace. It is grounded in truth and nourished by the tears of liberation our wise foremothers have shed. It flourishes in the rich soil of all you've overcome to reach this moment. No longer do you dwell in the shadows of others' narratives; you are now the author of your own story, where healing is the norm, safety is unwavering, and softness is revered.

That old story, the one that told you to be quiet, to be grateful, to endure, to be perfect, is over.

This is the beginning of your real life.
Your soft life.
Your whole life.

All you have to do is *Just Let Go.*

Explore what you're finally ready to release. What burdens no longer reflect who you are? What patterns, relationships, or beliefs have run their course? Letting go doesn't mean erasing the past; it means making room for what's next.

What kind of peace are you ready to welcome now?

Epilogue
A New Way to Be

There is a world waiting for us, not just imagined, but possible. A world where Black women are no longer defined by our endurance, our labor, or how quietly we carry our wounds. A world where we are not expected to prove our worth in systems designed to overlook us, where we are not constantly playing small to be accepted or embraced. A world where we are not just surviving, but living, laughing, expanding, and healing without shame.

This new way of being is not a finish line to cross. It is not a prize for perfection. It is not found in productivity, performance, or praise. It is a slow, sacred, deeply personal evolution. A remembering of what has always been true: we are already whole. Peace and happiness are not a reward for hard work; it's our birthright. We are allowed to be soft, seen, and celebrated, even in our stillness. No one really taught us this. We inherited stories of strength that required us to disappear inside them. We watched the women who came before us carry too much with too little, giving and giving until they vanished inside their roles. Somewhere along the way, we learned to do the same, but we are the ones who get to stop the cycle. We are the ones who get to say, "Not anymore."

This reclamation begins in the moments you whisper "no" instead of saying "yes." It's in the way you stop apologizing for your existence. It's in the breath, the emotional pause, you take before reacting. It's the way you rest without guilt. It's about letting yourself cry and not trying to suppress the emotion. It's the softness you extend toward your own heart; maybe for the first time.

I remember walking across the stage after completing my Doctoral program. It was important to me my kids were there to witness it. Out of my immediate family, I was the only one who'd ever achieved that goal. I shook the Dean's hand, walked out of the ceremony, and found my family waiting for me. Ava ran up first and said, "Mom, I need your cap and gown for my graduation." Phoenix followed right behind her, "Congratulations, Dr. Morrison," he said with a proud smile. They both wrapped their arms around me with such warmth and love I had to hold back tears. Later that night, Phoenix opened his school computer to catch up on work and glanced over at me. "Mom, what are you going to be working on next?" he asked. And that question stopped me in my tracks.

It dawned on me in that moment, my children had never seen me rest. They had seen the grind, the discipline, the sacrifice, the late nights, the ambition. They had seen me chase goal after goal, from military service to school to career. They had never seen me pause. They had never seen me breathe – and they needed to. "I'm going to rest," I replied. "Maybe garden. Enjoy not having schoolwork."

Later that night, in the quiet after doing the dishes, laundry, and laying everything out for the next day, I sat with his question again. I thought about what resting meant for me. All my life, I had been *doing*: mothering my siblings, joining the Air Force to prepare for my mother's homecoming, pursuing higher levels of education, and pouring my love into raising my children. I had been safeguarding, nurturing, and strategizing for as long as I can recall. I honestly didn't know what letting go looked like. I didn't know what it felt like not to carry something heavy. It was in that space, between the quiet ache and the longing to be free, that this book was born. Writing it became the very act of letting go. It became my way of learning what ease could feel like. It became my prayer for myself, and for every woman like me.

Envision waking up without the burden of putting on your mental armor, without the need to measure how to make yourself smaller, quieter, or more acceptable, even before brushing your teeth. Picture entering a space without the nagging thought of whether you're too much or not enough. Imagine a life where tenderness is freely given, where your worth is not tied to your productivity or the facade of strength you maintain. Visualize relationships that allow you to express your pain without shame and celebrate your joy without apology.

Imagine building a life rooted in ease, not ease as a luxury, but ease as a necessity. Joy as a compass, not an afterthought. Love as a sacred right, not as a transaction. We were never meant to live in emotional exile, be everything to everyone while denying ourselves. We are allowed to receive. We are allowed to take up space. We are allowed to bloom wildly and rest deeply. We are allowed to want more. To need more. To be more. And we don't have to wait another day.

Embracing freedom and growth involves releasing the conditioning that has shaped us: the guilt, the fear, and the need to prove ourselves. In this act of letting go, we open the door to freedom. We are not broken; we are continually evolving. We are not lagging behind; we are perfectly on schedule. We are not demanding too much; we are simply claiming what rightfully belongs to us.

Take what you need from these pages. Let them live in your bones. Carry them into your relationships, your rest, your decisions, your dreams. Let them echo in your laughter, in your softness, in the boundaries you draw and the beauty you embody. Leave behind what no longer serves you. You do not owe anyone a version of yourself that makes them comfortable but leaves you depleted. Write your own ending, or better yet, write your new beginning. You are ready. You are worthy. You are free.

Dear Reader,

If you've made it to this page, thank you. Truly. Thank you for walking this journey with me, for turning these pages, for sitting with your truth, for cracking open spaces in your heart that maybe no one else sees but you. That takes courage. It takes a kind of love that doesn't always have language but lives in every quiet choice you've made to keep going, to keep feeling, to keep returning to yourself. There is nothing small about that. In a world that rewards numbness and performance, your presence here is an act of deep devotion to your own becoming. I honor that.

I wrote this book not because I had all the answers, but because I, too, was carrying questions that refused to stay silent. Questions that kept knocking at my spirit, asking to be felt, witnessed, and spoken. I needed space to name what was sacred and still tender. I needed a place to explore the kind of healing that doesn't always show up with clarity or confidence, but with trembling hands and open hearts. This book became that place for me, and I hope for you, too. A space where healing could be honest. Messy. Nonlinear. Where survival didn't have to be the whole story. Where we could talk about what it means to soften without shame, to let go without guilt, and to remember without apology.

Like you, I have been tired in ways sleep couldn't touch. I have felt invisible in rooms where I was expected to shine. I have smiled when I was breaking and answered "I'm fine" out of habit, not truth. I have held too much, for too long, for too many. And in that holding, I forgot that I was allowed to be held, too. I've mistaken responsibility for worthiness. I've confused endurance with love. I've betrayed myself trying to prove I was unbreakable. And like you, I have also tasted something sweeter: freedom. Joy. Grace. The quiet kind. The kind that doesn't need to be earned. The kind that shows up when you stop negotiating your needs and start honoring your soul. That kind of freedom is not loud; it's lived.

I hope this book felt like sitting on a porch with a sisterfriend. I hope it met you in the stillness and reminded you you're not alone in your questions, in your ache, in your search for happiness. I hope it invites you to exhale the weight you've carried. To grieve what or who never held you. To celebrate the parts of you that survived, even when no one was clapping. I hope it gave you permission to be soft without apology, to be tired without guilt, and to be whole without needing to prove anything to anyone, not even yourself. To remember softness is not a disadvantage and letting go is not giving up; it's honoring your intuition, your peace, and embracing a self that doesn't need to beg for love. Healing is not about becoming someone new; it's about remembering who you were and putting in the work to grow spiritually, mentally, and emotionally. This takes grace, tenderness, self-love, and trust. It is challenging but it is worth it.

There's no perfect way to heal. No single map. No checklist or arrival point. Healing happens in layers. In pauses. In the way you speak to yourself on a hard morning, because words are powerful. These moments may seem small, but they are holy. What I know for sure is this: every time I choose myself with love, even quietly, a burden is lifted.

We embody both legacy and light. We are already whole—not at some point in the future, not after earning another degree, starting a new relationship, or reaching a new milestone. Our true essence radiates from deep within us this very moment, even amidst uncertainty, during transitional phases, and while we are still exploring our paths. Let this be your reminder, your reflection, and your invitation to reconnect with yourself. You are not falling behind. You are not broken. You are making progress, and, more importantly, you are growing in ways that may not always be visible but are profoundly transformative.

I see you. I celebrate you. And I'm walking beside you, not above, not ahead, but right here. With you. Still learning. Still softening. Still becoming. We don't need to have it all figured out to be worthy of peace. We just need to stay honest. Stay open. Stay rooted in love.

With all my love,
Jamie
Author of Just Let Go

Read More at

JAMIE MORRISON
BOOTS BIBS
& Barbells
JUST LET GO!
JAMIEJAI.COM